Mary

M000115522

"Multiculturalism is on everyone's lips these days, but we are still struggling with entrenched barriers that perpetuate exclusion and suspicion. This book shows us why diversity must be pursued along with hospitality, repentance, and justice. Tim Dickau warns us that the kingdom of God is no simple excursion and has provided a pilgrim's roadmap honed by prayer, failures, awkwardness, surprises, and, above all, abiding wisdom and lavish grace."

—Chris Lee

University of British Columbia

"This is definitely not one of those 'how to' books on church growth. It is for those who want to be challenged to move away from the isolation of individualism, the complacency of their comfort zone, and the use of God in a consumerist religion. It is for those who fear the different, those who are indifferent to the vulnerable, and those who harbor idolatries of all sorts.

"The book is easy to read, nonetheless the shared stories will pose a challenge to all who want to learn to be God's agent of hope and healing through His local churches."

—Amanda Shao Tan

Asian Theological Seminary, Manila, Philippine

"Over 20 years within a vibrant community of faith, Tim has lived the four trajectories that he calls all churches to in this book. It is a call to participate in God's liberating mandate of love by moving us to (1) radical hospitality, (2) shared life in diversity, (3) seeking justice for the least, and (4) embracing new life in Christ. Freedom is found there, shalom is found there. This is a book that begs to be read over and over. It is a book that leads us into deep living and identification with communities in which churches are placed. Most of all it is a book that emerges from years of laughter, tears, suffering, and joys as a church and its leaders live deeply into the neighborhood."

—Gary V. Nelson

President of Tyndale University College and Seminary

Author of *Borderland Churches*

PLUNGING INTO THE KINGDOM WAY

NML NEW MONASTIC LIBRARY
Resources for Radical Discipleship

For over a millennium, if Christians wanted to read theology, practice Christian spirituality, or study the Bible, they went to the monastery to do so. There, people who inhabited the tradition and prayed the prayers of the church also copied manuscripts and offered fresh reflections about living the gospel in a new era. Two thousand years after the birth of the church, a new monastic movement is stirring in North America. In keeping with ancient tradition, new monastics study the classics of Christian reflection and are beginning to offer some reflections for a new era. The New Monastic Library includes reflections from new monastics as well as classic monastic resources unavailable elsewhere.

Series Editor: Jonathan Wilson-Hartgrove

Plunging into the

KINGDOM WAY

Practicing the Shared Strokes
of Community, Hospitality,
Justice, and Confession

TIM DICKAU

With a foreword by
Charles Ringma

 CASCADE *Books* · Eugene, Oregon

PLUNGING INTO THE KINGDOM WAY
Practicing the Shared Strokes of Community, Hospitality, Justice, and Confession

New Monastic Library: Resources for Radical Discipleship 7

Cascade Books
An Imprint of Wipf and Stock Publishers
199 W. 8th Ave., Suite 3
Eugene, OR 97401

www.wipfandstock.com

ISBN 13: 978-1-60899-258-4

Cataloging-in-Publication data:

Dickau, Tim.

Plunging into the kingdom way : practicing the shared strokes of community, hospitality, justice, and confession / Tim Dickau ; foreword by Charles Ringma.

xvi + 142 p. ; 23 cm. —Includes bibliographical references.

New Monastic Library: Resources for Radical Discipleship 7

ISBN 13: 978-1-60899-258-4

1. Communities—Religious aspects—Christianity. 2. Christian life. I. Ringma, Charles. II. Title. III. Series.

BV4517.5 .D53 2011

Manufactured in the U.S.A.

To my wife Mary, our three boys, Thomas, Taylor and Mitchell,
and to all the people with whom we have taken up these shared practices

CONTENTS

In many ways the church in the Western world is struggling. Impacted by secular culture and having lost its way internally due to a lack of biblical, spiritual, and missional formation, the church is marked by consumer values. This means that many who attend church are only there to gain religious services from religious professionals. But there is little sense of being a faith community with a common life inviting high levels of ownership, relationship, and participation. As a consequence, there is little sense of commitment and people easily move on to worship elsewhere if there is something they don't like about their present church.

All of this is exacerbated by the highly mobile urban world in which we now find ourselves. Neighborhoods are highly transitional. People are on the move. We relocate for vocational, educational, and family and personal reasons. And so, many Western urban churches turn over most of their congregation in a five-year period. This hardly augurs well for spiritual formation, training in leadership, sustaining ministries, and building community.

This is further complicated by the fact that neighborhoods change due to gentrification or deterioration. As a result members of the church move to better parts of the city when their neighborhood changes for the worse or they have to move because they can no longer afford to live there due to spiraling housing costs. This adds to the instability of many churches. Little wonder, therefore, that many Christians in Western churches feel themselves to be more like religious refugees rather than members of the household of faith.

It is within this broad picture frame that we need to read the story of Grandview Calvary Baptist church in East Vancouver, Canada, in its recent journey of revitalization and reconfiguration. Twenty years ago this church with its small remaining and aging, but faithful, congregation looked as if it was ready for the funeral dirge. Instead it sang the songs of hope and resurrection. It is this church's movement towards new life that forms the substance of this book. As such, this is a story of hope for the Western church—a story that is still being written in this challenging part of the city of Vancouver.

While every story, like a tapestry, is multi-colored and multi-layered, this story too has many themes and melodies. A stark distillation includes some of the following dimensions that brought about renewal:

- a vision of the Reign or Kingdom of God
- biblical preaching and teaching
- empowering leadership
- integrated worship
- regular pastoral care
- spiritual formation
- healing practices
- neighbourhood presence
- community building
- creative use of the arts
- serving the poor
- commitment to the work of justice

It is important, however, that the above is not read as a how-to list. The above are not steps to having a successful church. That is not how revitalization and renewal take place. It is far more complex. There are the mysterious workings of the renewing Spirit. There are the hidden hours of prayer. There are the small steps of faith. There are the tentative new projects. There is the willingness to experiment. There are the quiet surrenders, the voluntary relinquishments, and sacrificial commitments to act. There is the practice of welcome. There is careful discernment.

Furthermore, there is the willingness to hang in and the courage to take seemingly impossible steps. And there are the leaders, the formators, the carers, the evangelists, those with financial resources, the visionaries, the administrators and the many who are willing to do the many humble acts of service. All of this is the mysterious intertwining of God's presence with human receptivity and creativity. This is the mysterious working of the body of Christ—the community of faith bound together in worship, relationship, and the work of the kingdom of God.

A number of themes, however, call for further elaboration.

The first is the significance of the recovery of the older concept of parish church. This is church as the people of God in Christ living in a particular neighborhood for which they assume a priestly and missional responsibility. This means that many of the people who worship at Grandview Calvary Baptist church live in the neighborhood where the church building is located. Many walk to church. This is their turf. And many have deliberately relocated into the neighborhood to be part of the church's communal life and mission.

This is church as incarnational presence in a particular part of the city. This vision of being the people of God forms a stark contrast to the familiar and more prevalent concept of commuter church. A church building is located in the neighborhood, but the faith community is not. The church as the body of Christ in a particular neighborhood echoes the old Benedictine idea of the vow of stability. In its contemporary outworking this means that one commits oneself to continue to be part of the life and mission of a particular church. This may well mean that one then says no to a job transfer and no to relocation when the neighborhood deteriorates. Being an on-going part of the mission of that particular church takes precedence over other considerations. This is a commitment to particularity for the sake of the gospel.

The second challenging theme is that of building community. This comes to expression at the Grandview church in many ways. It involves connecting with the neighborhood. It includes building relationships within the life of the church. It is expressed in working together in a whole range of projects, including the missional projects of the church among which are also various income-generating projects. And it includes the formation of a number of intentional Christian communities (ICCs) that provide a safe place for political refugee claimants and those needing support in their journey towards wholeness.

Of particular note is the formation of ICCs. And here the Grandview church charts a new course. In the 1960s and 70s many ICCs came into being. But most were disconnected from the Protestant and Evangelical church. At Grandview it was the parish church that spawned the ICCs connected to the church. And like the much older tradition in Christianity of a symbiotic relationship between the parish church and monastic communities and religious orders living a communal life, Grandview also reflects a productive relationship between church and the ICCs. The ICCs are seen as deepening the life of the parish church and bringing to keener expression that the whole people of God are to live the koinonia of the Trinity. Furthermore, ICCs can further the mission of the church particularly in the practice of radical hospitality. The church continues to explore other ways of forming ICCs as an ongoing expression of the idea that the church is to be a hermeneutic of the gospel. What this means is that church as herald, servant, and sacrament of the Reign of God can not only say "hear the word" but also "come and see the word of God made flesh amongst us."

A third important theme in the inviting and challenging Grandview church story, is the growing practice of the spiritual disciplines and the formation of a communal spirituality. In worship, teaching and sacraments, and in prayer retreats, healing practices, meditation, the creative use of the arts, the quiet use of the charismatic gifts, the composition of songs and prayers and poetry which are used communally, a spirituality in Christ through the Spirit is being forged which reflects the much older traditions of the Christian church.

And lastly, this neighborhood church is a missional community of faith. Work projects for marginalized people, services for refugee claimants, after school programs, services for single moms and a regular weekly meal for the homeless are only some of the many projects which express the desire to bring God's shalom into the neighborhood.

So I want to invite you into reading this story of this untypical Baptist church—a church that has moved beyond the stereotypical forms that were primarily shaped in the years after the 1950s. This story is of a church that seeks to be part of the twenty-first century and not a relic of the past. Yet at the same time this community of faith seeks to draw on the wider traditions of the Christian church, including its spiritual practices and its forms of community.

Dr. Tim Dickau, one of the key pastors of the church, is serving the wider church well in telling this telling story. While he would never say, "Replicate what we have done at Grandview," he would say, "Please use this story as a source of hope for what God can yet do in the empowering of the Western church for first-world re-evangelization and for the transformation of our Western way of life in order to reflect more of the Gospel way of life and for the healing of our torn social fabric."

Charles Ringma,
theologian and social activist

ACKNOWLEDGMENTS

The journey I describe in this book has been a shared one from the beginning. With the first seventy or eighty people who were part of Grandview Calvary Baptist to the numerous folks who have joined along the way, we have navigated these rapids and learned these strokes in one big canoe. I want to thank you all for climbing in the boat and paddling along. There really are too many folks to begin mentioning some of you by name because I know I will leave too many out. Thanks for loving me and giving me room to learn how to lead and follow during the moments when you were left shaking your heads, confused about where I was going.

I want to thank Carey Theological College for the latitude to write a narrative thesis for my Doctor of ministry project. I especially want to thank Jonathan Wilson, my supervisor, and Barbara Mutch for their patience while I was trying to figure out what to do next at Grandview and paying very little attention to finishing that project. The occasional kick in the butt helped focus me on my writing. I also want to thank Karen Wuest, my very capable editor, who continues to live out and embody the vision of our church with her family.

I want to thank all the people who have lived in our house over the last twenty years. Every one of you has taught me more about myself. The gift of sharing life together has far outweighed the exasperating moments. We truly have been enrolled in "the school of love."

Lastly, I want to thank my family. Our three boys, Thomas, Taylor, and Mitchell, have been willing participants in this journey, even though they didn't initially sign up for it. Playing soccer and hockey, wrestling, talking, reading, arguing and hanging out with you has kept me honest and hopeful. To see you each take up this way of life in your own way and to contribute to our own experience of community and hospitality has brought some of the biggest smiles to my face. Thanks guys. I am truly grateful for each of you.

Mary and I got married pretty young according to today's Western cultural standards. Getting married early means that you get the opportunity to grow up together. I think we have done that. At times, it has also meant that we have wounded each other. Gratefully, we both have come to know God's healing power, personally and together. Learning to find our stroke together has been and continues to be a great adventure. I'm looking forward to the rest of the journey with you, my love.

ONE

Getting Ready for the Ride

During my fourteenth summer, I went on a canoe trip with ten other teens on the Little Smokey River, a Northern Canadian waterway that we expected would require little more than a steady paddle. To our surprise, that tributary had rapids, which sprayed water over the tops of our canoes. Over half our supplies were lost in our first spill, an experience that stretched our creativity and inspired us to "rapidly" learn new strokes. While we had plenty of mishaps, my paddling partners and I eventually developed a common rhythm in our strokes that enabled us to navigate those turbulent waters. After four days on the Little Smokey, we met up with the larger Peace River, our destination, where we met others who had also journeyed on the wild Smokey. As we shared stories of discovery, I began to see that our adventure was part of a larger movement of people who were being initiated into this ancient but contemporary craft of river riding.

As a pastor for more than twenty years at the Grandview Calvary Baptist Church (GCBC) community in Vancouver, British Columbia, I now see that the journey I took in that canoe so many years ago resembles the disorienting ride that many churches—including ours—have taken in trying to stay afloat through the waves of change that have swept over our culture (the fizzling of Christendom,[1] the shift towards post-modernism,[2] and the accompanying ideological fragmentation,[3] to name just a few).

1. For example, see Newbigin, *Foolishness to the Greeks*.

2. For example, see Walsh and Middleton, *Truth is Stranger than it Used to Be*.

3. For example, see MacIntyre, *After Virtue*. See also. Wilson, *Living Faithfully in a Fragmented World*.

Yet amidst these rapids, God is stirring the church—ours as well as many others who have paddled through the same rough waters—to articulate ancient but contemporary strokes, or practices, that will usher His people towards the final destination: the river of peace that is the Kingdom of God.[4]

I have described these practices as four trajectories, which call upon the church to participate in the mission of God by moving: (1) from isolation to community towards radical hospitality; (2) from homogeneity to diversity towards shared life among cultures; (3) from charity to friendship towards seeking justice for the least; (4) from the confrontation of idolatries to repentance towards new life in Christ. These practices shape us according to God's reign and liberate us from enslavement to the powerful forces of our dominant Western culture.[5] Many theologians and authors have served as cartographers, helping to map the numerous rapids that our church has navigated in its turbulent river ride.[6]

By sharing the story of our particular church's attempt to pursue these common practices over the last two decades, I hope to offer fellow paddlers our own chart through these transforming, exhilarating and choppy waters of change and so bear witness to the rearranged world that Jesus inaugurated. Though we are still on the journey, the imagination of our church community has been enlarged along the way, and together, we both "see the world as it is yet . . . look beyond it to a world with God's will done, God's kingdom come."[7]

---

4. For examples, see Bass and Volf, *Practicing Theology*; Rutba House, *School(s) for Conversion*; Bass, *Christianity for the Rest of Us*.

5. See Guder, *Continuing Conversion of the Church*, for the need for the church to renew its participation in the mission of God. Lesslie Newbigin sounded the warning of the Western Church's enslavement to modernism over two decades ago in *Foolishness to the Greeks*.

6. This book is an adaptation of my Doctor of Ministry Thesis at Carey Theological College. My investigation of our development as a church relied heavily on personal testimony, both testimony garnered from pastoral work and from my interviews with those who have led us in these movements. The fourteen interviews I undertook with individuals and groups from our church gave shape to my understanding of these movements. While I also investigated documented evidence such as newsletters, reports, minutes, reflections and sermons, much of the substance of this narrative comes from my own personal observations and reflections.

7. Storie, "Imagination, Justice and the Spirit of God," 69.

My prayer is that you, fellow paddlers, might also be inspired to take up these ancient but newly shaped practices, in whatever tributary you might find yourself, as you continue on your own journey toward the great river of God's kingdom.

TWO

Navigating the Rapids of Isolation, Fragmentation, and Transience

To be rooted is perhaps the most important and least recognized need of the human soul. It is one of the hardest to define. A human being has roots by virtue of his real, active and natural participation in the life of a community which preserves in living shape certain particular treasures of the past and certain particular expectations for the future.[1]

I wonder if the days of "going to church" might be vanishing faster than VCR's from our North American cultural landscape. Numbed by secular powers such as individualism, consumerism and ideological fragmentation, many of today's generation are longing to counteract these secular powers and forge a new way of being the church. Over the past twenty years, as I have pastored our urban church on the northwest edge of this continent, I have discovered that people from radically different backgrounds share this in common: they are tired of being isolated and are longing for community. Despite the pull within us towards autonomy, the longing for a shared life has kept pulling us together. The movement from isolation to community towards radical hospitality has been the primary trajectory of our church. But we didn't start there.

My first encounter with the people of GCBC came at a church retreat held in the winter of 1989. During our conversations, several people ex-

1. Weil, *Need for Roots*, 41.

pressed nostalgia for the strong sense of community that had been present in the church during the late 1970s and early 1980s, when church membership had been at a hundred and fifty and the congregation had been thriving. Among the thirty people gathered for the retreat, a second feature emerged: the congregation functioned with what one member described as "sanctuary friendliness," where people related to each other for the gathering of worship but were not involved in each other's daily lives. Third, like so many urban churches in North American cities,[2] the congregation was isolated and disengaged from the neighborhood surrounding the church building due to the geographical dispersing of many members, especially the young adults who had left ten or twenty years earlier in search of cheaper housing. With a dwindling congregation of only fifty or sixty people, most of whom were seniors and few of whom lived in the neighborhood, the church had lost a vision for the future and *"the goal was just to stay alive."*[3]

With the declining membership and a sanctuary building in disrepair, our congregation questioned whether they had a future in the neighborhood, or if they should dissolve, like the dozen other neighborhood churches that had left or died in the previous three decades. Disconnected from the people of the Grandview-Woodlands neighborhood,[4] one longtime GCBC member said that the church *"lived with a mentality that the people* [in our neighborhood] *weren't interested: they are all Italians and Catholic who have their own church and do their own thing. I don't remember any attempt to find out who else was out there."*

Early on, I surmised that our church would have to "die" to our past "glory" as a church if we were to move down the new and uncharted waters before us. As the chair of the deacons put it in his report at the end of 1988, *"we are not sure at this time what our approach will be to the community but we know we must do something* [if we are to survive]." We were at a crossroads that many churches at the end of Christendom have

2. See Bakke, *Urban Christian*, 46.

3. Quotations from congregants of GCBC are in italics while all other quotations are not, except some of those at the beginning of a new section. Interviewees are identified by number.

4. Our church building is located at the corner of the main thoroughfare in the Grandview-Woodlands neighborhood and one block east of the Commercial Drive business district.

had to face: Would we continue on as a chaplaincy supporting the present members until their death? Or would we face this death, which after all is so entwined in the story of Jesus, and share in the larger mission of Christ by living out the gospel in our changing neighborhood?

At the same time, I came to realize that the people of the Grandview-Woodlands neighborhood no longer saw much value in the Christian church. Many people in our neighborhood were unfamiliar with the churches and perceived very little social benefit from their presence. Thirty-three percent of the population in this neighborhood identified themselves as having "no religion" in the 1981 census, which was one of the highest figures in all of Canada.[5] Many of the residents I spoke with had embraced the post-modern suspicion of Christian faith and actually perceived churches as deficits. One woman who worked at the community center focused on Christianity as the cause of many of society's problems: clerical abuse, mistreatment of aboriginal people, environmental devastation, intolerance and discrimination towards people who were gay or single parents. Indeed, the trends toward secularism that have affected all of North America have accelerated here in our context, making Vancouver, and our neighborhood in particular, a sort of laboratory for discerning the church's response to this emerging reality all over the Western world.[6]

Moreover, our church's growing isolation and disconnection from the neighborhood followed the trend in North American society towards atomization,[7] a shift that coincided with a decrease in Canadian church attendance.[8] In his magisterial work on the sources that form our conception of the person, Charles Taylor presents a genealogy through the broad sweep of human history, observing how humans have moved from a corporate identity into a predominately individualistic identity, focusing

---

5. The figure for Canada with "no religion" was 7.3 percent. See *Statistics Canada*. (1981).

6. In 1995, Ray Bakke commented to me that Vancouver was a laboratory of "North America's future."

7. Putnam, "Bowling Alone," 65–78. Quentin Schultze observes how much human communication is now mediated by technology instead of face to face dialogue in *Habits of the High-Tech Heart*.

8. Monthly attendance dropped from 41 percent in 1975 to 37 percent in 1980 and to 30 percent in 2000, as reported in Jim Coggins, "State of the Canadian Church: A Nation of Believers?" 1–2.

particularly on how we have accelerated our move towards individualism in Western culture since the Reformation and Renaissance.[9] Along with so many other churches, we found ourselves wondering how we could recover a genuine communal Christianity when up against the strong isolating and atomizing forces of our culture, particularly when, as Zygmunt Bauman observes, "the decline of community is . . . self-perpetuating; once it takes off, there are fewer and fewer stimuli to stem the disintegration of human bonds and seek ways to tie again what has been torn apart."[10]

But it is into this culture of isolation that the gospel of Jesus Christ announces that God calls us from our isolation into community. Throughout the narrative of Scripture, the forming of a community for the sake of the world is at the heart of God's vision.[11] Jesus forms a community of itinerant disciples and leaves behind small groups in the villages he visits, calling them to implement his way of being the people of God, promising that his presence will abide wherever two or three are gathered in his name (Matt 18:20). The apostle Peter, writing to foreigners, slaves and women—people who were marginalized in that society—declares to them that they have become part of a holy people, chosen by God: "Once you were not a people but now you are God's people; once you had not received mercy, but now you have received mercy" (1 Pet 2:10).[12] If this call to community is integral to the church's life and witness, then isolated Christianity, contrary to the notions of "religion a la carte" so prominent in Canada[13] and many other countries, is an oxymoron.

---

9. Taylor, *Sources of the Self*. This movement towards individualism does not mean that these periods of history were by nature more compassionate or virtuous but that people situated their identity more firmly within a communal context. Nor does this imply that this is an entirely negative move; one only need consider the gains in human rights during the past two centuries as one example of a positive resulting from this trend towards individualism.

10. Bauman, *Community*, 48.

11. Wright, *Evil and the Justice of God*, 47–74.

12. See Elliot, *Home for the Homeless*, 59–88. for a description of the recipients of the Epistle.

13. See Bibby, *Fragmented Gods*.

FROM ISOLATION TO COMMUNITY

> *Welcome is one of the signs that a community is alive. To invite
> others to live with us is a sign that we aren't afraid, that we have
> a treasure of truth and of peace to share . . . A community which
> refuses to welcome—whether through fear, weariness, insecurity, a
> desire to cling to comfort, or just because it is fed up with visitors—is
> dying spiritually.*[14]

One factor that altered our sense of isolation as individuals in our
church was the arrival of a number of international students who moved
into the neighborhood and showed up one Sunday to participate in the
church's worship. Their presence, and the fact that their arrangements for
room and board required them to be back by noon for lunch, compelled a
couple of members to offer a shared lunch in the church building following worship. According to one member, this lunch began to foster renewed
relationships among the long-time worshippers as well as the newcomers. There were roughly sixty people in the congregation at this time. The
presence of the stranger, while often perceived as a threat to our settled
lives, can be God's means to awaken within us the call to welcome others.
Welcoming the stranger also reminds us of God's initiative in welcoming
us, while we were not only strangers to him, but opposed to him (Rom
5:8–10). Jesus likens our welcome of the stranger in need to our welcome
of him (Matt 25:40), adding a new dimension to all of our encounters
with the stranger. Even though these newcomers found and joined the
church without an intentional welcome, they stirred up the welcome of
God in our congregation. They were the catalyst for the flourishing of one
woman's ministry with children and teens in particular.

When Mary and I arrived in 1989 to engage the church in a six-
month study of the Grandview-Woodlands neighborhood,[15] our arrival
also stirred up hope in the congregation, particularly since we decided
to live in the neighborhood, just six blocks from the church. At the time,
this choice to live in the neighborhood ran counter to the aspirations of
many congregants, who aspired to leave the neighborhood for economic

14. Vanier, *Community and Growth,* 268.

15. The church leadership had agreed to partner with the denomination in calling me,
a newly graduated seminary student, to study the neighborhood as part of the church's
discernment process.

(cheaper or larger housing) and social (better neighborhood) reasons. While living within the locale of the church building seemed to us like the inevitable choice if we were going to get to know the place, it was not a choice made easily. Before we had made that decision, Mary and I had driven down Commercial Drive one afternoon, and Mary had pointed toward the decaying buildings, unkempt retail outlets and strangely out-fitted characters and declared, "I sure wouldn't want to live here." But six months later, we found ourselves moving within one-half block of the very place where Mary had made that comment. In hindsight, we took this as God's way of teaching us to love this neighborhood, these run-down buildings, and these "strange" neighbors. We were being called to face our fears and typecasting, to discover our common humanity with those who disturbed us so that we might come near to them.

Community and Theology of Place

That decision to live in Grandview-Woodlands was pivotal in learning to be at home in and, later, to love our neighborhood. It is difficult to imag-ine how we could have developed the sort of natural networks and shared life together we did if we had lived in a distant part of the city, something I discovered many of the clergy whose churches were in our neighborhood had chosen to do. It is equally difficult to imagine how smaller churches like GCBC can overcome the fragmentation so intrinsic to our culture and begin to live out of a kingdom vision without sharing in the life of the neighborhood.[16] For incoming clergy, choosing to live in the neighbor-hood of the church building declares that they are willing to embrace this particular place, an expression of incarnation reverberating from Christ.

A particular encouragement for us during this period was the arrival of a family who moved a few blocks away from us, intentionally locating in this neighborhood. Since many of our neighbors would have preferred to relocate to a better neighborhood, having a family move there who had chosen this area because they wanted to live in a part of the city that had

16. For a description of the fragmentation of our ethical world(s), see Wilson, *Living Faithfully in a Fragmented World*, 24–38. Sociologically, urban life is also fragmented geographically in that many folks work in one neighborhood, shop in another, meet friends in a third, worship in a fourth, etc. I will explore this theme of living in a neigh-borhood as part of a church in greater depth in a later section.

social warts gave us a greater sense of developing a team.[17] Even a few committed people can begin to spark a fire within an entire community.

Over time, instead of merely "living here," Mary and I—and many others in our congregation—have come to indwell this place, developing a shared experience, concern and involvement that has woven our narrative, and the narrative of this neighborhood, together into a new story. Walter Bruggemann aptly describes what happens when people live hospitably in a place: "Place is space which has historical meanings, where some things have happened which are now remembered and which provide continuity and identity across generations. Place is space in which important words have been spoken, which have established identity, defined vocation, and envisioned destiny."[18]

If we are to overcome the fragmentation of contemporary life and contribute to the stewardship of creation within our cities, we need to recover an understanding of how God is restoring and redeeming places rather than discarding them. We must ask what that restorative work means for our own care of public buildings, trees, sidewalks, church buildings and houses. When you inhabit and embrace a place over the long haul, the descriptions of Shalom found in Scripture—a culture in which humans flourish, relationships are restored and creation moves towards completion—become more imaginable. For our church, this has meant experiencing a number of beneficial outcomes, including the natural intersection of people in daily life, the development of community, the ability to imagine Shalom taking root in this neighborhood, increased cooperation with other churches and neighborhood groups, and the recovery of a theology of place. By recovering a theology of place, we have gained peepholes into God's kingdom vision of a world of beauty, justice, relationships and spiritual vitality.

Our church's commitment to root in a particular place has created tension between those who live in the neighborhood and those who live outside of it. As a woman whom I perceive to be in the center of our mission confided to me, "*Those of us who live outside the neighborhood feel like outsiders.*" And it's true that those who live outside the neighbor-

---

17. Relocating to the abandoned places of the empire is one of the marks of new monasticism, as well as one of John Perkins's three R's of community development.

18. Bruggemann, *The Land: Place as Gift*, 5.

hood do not experience the same level of natural connections: "*I think probably [community] is quite good for anybody who lives near the church, because even if I go down there to shop, I bump into this one, that one, and the other one. It is more than just seeing people in church, it is part of the community.*"

While living in close proximity to the community does lead to a rich experience of being the church, we are grappling with what it means for us to be a neighborhood-focused church as people who live in different neighborhoods are attracted to our holistic vision and also as some who have been living in the neighborhood are forced to move further out in search of affordable housing due to the inflationary thrust in the housing market of Grandview-Woodlands over the past several years. One congregant notes the costly choices many people have made in resisting taking up residence elsewhere for economic reasons.

> *[Twenty years ago] young people would not have been satisfied to stick around. I am so amazed at our young people . . . willing to live in a basement suite or rent a part of a home. [Back then] you just moved further out and to the same kind of you're your parents had.*

How we respond to these tensions will be important to our church's future. Undoubtedly, as neighborhoods experience transformation, all who have relocated to "abandoned places of the empire" will face this tension.[19]

Perhaps the most significant factor in reconnecting with the neighborhood and contributing to the sense of community has been the individual contributions of people who live, work and participate in neighborhood issues and who are known as part of the church. Over the years, the number of residents who were also congregants increased. Those local congregants gained a kingdom vision and pursued involvements around a multitude of neighborhood issues. One home group with members who lived adjacent to each other hosted a few block parties, gathering together people who for the most part didn't know each other. Furthermore, our church has become known as a "community church," as a people who are of and for Grandview-Woodlands.

Living, working, shopping, using services, engaging in recreation, hanging out and participating in a common neighborhood all bring a new

---

19. See Rutba House, *School(s) of Conversion*.

level of integration into our fragmented lives. Interconnections emerge which give people a greater sense of being known and rooted, reweaving isolated, fragmented lives into a healthier whole. These interconnections—unplanned, serendipitous and transforming—lead to stability and fraternity.[20] So much of the goodness of GCBC, at least for those who live and/or work in Grandview-Woodlands, comes from this geographical proximity and shared sense of a village.

Not only are relationships deepened and enhanced through sharing a common neighborhood, our vision for and participation in the neighborhood changes, too. When you inhabit a neighborhood together as part of a community, you begin to grasp a kingdom vision of God's inbreaking into our neighborhoods, a biblical vision for a city of delight, full of gardens and beauty and creativity, a place where justice for the least and joyful celebration exist side by side.[21] When you inhabit a place as part of a community, you not only draw energy from one another to be involved in cultivating these characteristics, but you also begin to care about this place, your home, where you dwell with neighbors you have come to care about and even love as you share life together. If you work in one place, shop in another, play in a third and "go to church" (which is bad theology to begin with) in a fourth, life becomes more fragmented. When you are part of a community that inhabits a neighborhood with a vision to be involved in its transformation, life itself becomes more integrated and whole. Our communities become kinder, and we begin to consider each other's welfare as we make economic, social, and political decisions.

Being a neighborhood pastor also moves us from a professional, distanced role to one where we nurture relationships based on our common humanity in the natural flow of life. So much of my pastoral work takes place "on the go" as I encounter people on the street, meet them at a party or meeting in the neighborhood, or end up praying with them impromptu at one of our programs. One morning, as I was heading home from my exercise routine at the gym, I encountered John, a homeless man who struggles with addiction but manages to hold down a full-time job. Arranging for an "appointment" to meet with John is difficult, but when

20. This theme of a community situated in a place, a neighborhood, is another theme I will explore in the conclusion.

21. Wolterstorff, *Until Justice and Peace Embrace*, 124–40.

I saw him on the street at 7:30 that morning, I offered him a ride to the Skytrain station and we talked in the car for twenty minutes. After I had breakfast and prayers with my family, I went for coffee at my usual café, where the barista I was getting to know well asked me about my church (and showed up for worship the next weekend). As I sat down in my regular spot to review my day and pray, I saw a woman walk by and invited her in to continue a conversation we had begun two weeks previously. All this took place before I "started work" in the natural flow of my day.

Community and Transformation of Place

But in those formative years, even as we sought to love our neighborhood and the people of our congregation, we still faced major difficulties as we sought to rebuild community, difficulties typical of many inner-city churches. When we first arrived, we discovered that three of the eight classrooms in the church building were filled with garbage, most of the floors in those rooms were rotten and the paint and carpet were fit for the dump. Much of my first year was spent doing construction, working on renovations along with others from our church, a task which definitely humbled me given my inadequateness to the task. As we completed these renovations together, however, we also got more acquainted and developed capacity for cooperative action.

Another challenge was the increasing level of festering conflict, centered upon issues of leadership and changes being implemented to connect with the neighborhood. The arrival of a senior couple who were well known in the denomination and who chose to join our church upon their return to Vancouver reassured the congregation, especially the seniors, that these changes were moving in the right direction.

Lesslie Newbigin sounded the warnings a few decades ago that a church could develop a thriving community with all sorts of programs and activities and yet leave the surrounding neighborhood and culture untouched.[22] Not wanting to make this same mistake when I first arrived at GCBC, I interviewed residents, merchants, educators, politicians and social servants and quickly discovered that the church was unknown. If the gospel was going to be heard as surprising, good news, then I knew

22. Newbiggin, *Foolishness to the Greeks*, 85.

that our church had to demonstrate that we were devoted to the welfare of our neighborhood.[23]

One of my own first involvements was to participate in the monthly gathering of neighborhood health, education, and social servants (the Grandview-Woodlands Area Services Team). My foray into this committee raised a few eyebrows, but over the years people realized that I was not a fundamentalist and that I wanted to contribute as a partner in seeking human flourishing in our neighborhood.[24]

Developing church programs that served identified needs in the neighborhood furthered that trust, as did our commitment to offering our services without an expectation that people participate in our worship.[25] Our initial programmatic responses to building community with our neighbors included a children's summer day camp, a children's midweek program, and "Parent's Morning Out," a weekly program for parents at home with pre-school children to meet others, receive childcare (for which I was the primary and unskilled caregiver), listen to a speaker about parenting, relationship or neighborhood issues, and participate in discussion. About ten parents became a regular part of this group in the first year.

The development of this group also met a need in our own lives: as new parents, we longed for more friends our own age who were also parents, a group which was absent from our church at the time. While we were developing good relations with the seniors of our congregation and some of the teens, there were very few couples or families. The men and women who became part of this group precipitated our own movement as parents from isolation into community. One woman joined the group after we began talking about our parental isolation and loneliness while our children played at the park.

---

23. Wright, *Surprised by Hope*, 232. "Of course, evangelism will flourish best if the church is giving itself to works of justice . . . and works of beauty."

24. That growing trust was reflected in the committee's appointment of me as co-chair eight years later.

25. When I led a group of seminary students on a neighborhood tour and we stopped to chat with one of the respected counsellors in Grandview-Woodlands, someone asked her whether she was open to working with faith groups. She responded by saying that she generally didn't refer people to faith groups but did refer people to our church's programs because she trusted Mary and me and she felt that we wouldn't proselytize her referrals.

Christine Pohl states that experiences such as ours "remind practitioners daily that the gifts of hospitality do not flow in one direction only; hospitality is a two-way street."[26] You could say that in extending invitation to our neighbor, God welcomes us. This sort of mutuality reflects Jesus' own ministry. In asking the disciples to pray for him in the Garden of Gethsemane, Jesus invites those whom he has called and taught to care for him at a time in his life when he needed their support. This perspective freed us to develop a more human way of life, rather than merely trying to get more church members to help the church survive.

A significant event occurred with this group about a year after it began which signaled that this movement towards community, though slight and slow, was happening. That Halloween, as Mary and I went out trick-or-treating with our one-year-old son, we made our way north in our neighborhood, picking up one, then two, then three of the families along the way, all unarranged liaisons. As we meandered through the neighborhood, we eventually arrived at our local community center, which was hosting a celebration with food and fireworks. We took pictures of our children, then stayed together, joking, laughing, and telling stories. After about twenty minutes, the executive director of the community center asked about our group. When I told him that we were a parents' group from our church, he nodded—though he was not connected to any church— and said to me, "Tim, keep at that. This is exactly the type of community building we need in this neighborhood." As he gave his prophetic word to me, I glanced around to survey the faces in the crowd of three hundred and noticed that ours was the only smaller group gathered. Given that we felt like our fledgling group of parents was tenuously connected, the director's words served both as an encouragement and a sign that community was beginning to form. As a number of the parents and spouses/partners of this group became believers and part of the church over the next year, we could see for ourselves the community-forming power of the gospel. Moreover, as each of these concrete expressions of care developed, we increasingly became, in the words of the community health coordinator, one of the "major partners in the community's well-being."[27]

---

26. Pohl, *Making Room*, 72.

27. Over time, after perceiving needs in the community, we began to offer year-round tutoring for children, leadership training for teens, support for single mothers, food and

Community and Transience

While no one left our church congregation because of conflict in those early years, which was a great sign of hope in itself, we did have several (of the very few) couples and students in our congregation relocate to new cities in 1992, less than three years after we had moved into the neighborhood. In a fledgling congregation of about seventy people, with its recent history of seeing young people move away, the departures of these friends seemed monumental, and I was depressed most of that fall.

Yet while we grieved the loss of those friends, we were also learning one of the key lessons of hospitality arising from a biblical vision. As Christine Pohl observes, "biblical hospitality differed from ancient hospitality in Roman society in that it was to be offered without thought for gain or reciprocity."[28] That is not to say that people who are welcomed are not invited or challenged by the call of the gospel to share in the responsibility of extending this welcome themselves, lest we create a stark division between those who welcome and the welcomed. Rather, the lesson being taught us was that hospitality is a gift we receive from God in Christ and are encouraged to offer others as an act of grace. We would eventually encapsulate this truth in the first part of our most recent vision statement: "GCBC is a community of people who receive and extend the radical welcome of God in Christ for the transformation of neighborhood."

By seeking to extend the welcome of God in Christ to all whom God brought into our community, we also sought to develop a "sending" philosophy, as a way of affirming the calling and responsibility of those relocating in other cities or countries to take our developing vision of the kingdom with them and embody it elsewhere. Those (now numerous) members who have moved away have expressed how much they valued this mission-minded response to their departure. Three years ago, Council affirmed the continued development of this sending vocation as part of a strategic plan. For small churches that are struggling to survive, this sending philosophy seems almost too difficult to practice. But by concretely naming that the seeds of the Kingdom that God is planting in our

shelter for our street population, social enterprises for people with barriers to employment, and affordable community housing.

28. Pohl, *Making Room*, 13.

world are much larger than our tiny ventures, our trust in God grew. And we came to recognize that the church is a force in the world.

That doesn't lessen the impact, however, of the grieving that goes with transience, particularly the type that unreflectively buys into the (upward) mobility of our culture. Mary and I faced this temptation ourselves: should we look for a bigger, better church with higher pay in a city where housing was more affordable? Many days, I checked the "pastoral postings" and flirted with sending resumes to those churches. During the discouragement and struggle of those early years, Eugene Peterson's call to the disciplines of prayer and theological reflection in the midst of everyday pastoral work[29] became a lifeline, helping me to recognize the incremental steps people were making towards God and community, even though nothing seemed to be "happening."

For the first decade, we agonized over these questions, as many in our community have since—and as countless other pastors and church leaders have who have paddled through similar turbulent waters. But I believe our choice to stay was critical. For when we finally stopped comparing our church to the large churches around us and chose to believe that God had given us people and resources to offer new life among us, we were prepared to consider first what God was calling us towards in this city, and then forsake an identity rooted in "career success" and work out issues of affordability with creative courage, trusting in God to supply our needs.

Israel Galindo, in his work of spiritual direction with pastors and congregations, contends that an entire decade is usually required for a pastor and congregation to develop the sort of trusting relationship required to move into a creative vision.[30] One of the questions confronting many pastors in similar churches is whether they are willing to live through these initial years of struggle in order to build the trust and presence required to lead the church to renewal.

While there are good, legitimate and God-ordained reasons for moving from one city, neighborhood, or church to another, I am convinced

---

29. Peterson, *Contemplative Pastor.*

30. Galindo, "Staying Put: A Look at the First Ten Years of Ministry." Galindo describes the typical life cycle for church and pastor in each of these ten years. His description matches my own experience with startling accuracy.

that each church's life and mission will lead to greater community and neighborhood transformation if more people who are part of the church make the choice to stay long-term in one particular place. A number of folks in our community have suggested that the next step, at least for some of us, is to make a vow of stability along the lines of the Benedictine monks. This commitment to root ourselves in a neighborhood for the long haul for the well-being of that particular place contrasts with the life of individual pursuit, where we are only concerned for our own well-being, or the flourishing of our own family or community. St. Benedict had little use for those who went from one community to another with self-serving intents. Speaking of "Landlopers," those who keep going their whole life from one province to another, Benedict writes: "Always roving and never settled, they indulge their passions and the cravings of their appetite."[31] I think that vows of stability could be revolutionary for the church's mission in our transient urban world.[32] Not only would they compel us to learn the graces of forgiveness and agape love in community, they would also urge us to move beyond acts of charity to seek more systemic change as we commit ourselves to being re-formed as communities with a vision for participating in the new world Jesus came to inaugurate.

FROM COMMUNITY TOWARD SHARED LIFE

What really turned the tide toward re-establishing community in the Grandview-Woodlands neighborhood—and eventually moving us towards more radical hospitality—was the development of a shared life rooted in the gospel. In order to move in that direction, we had to intentionally resist some of the cultural forces that have created and perpetuated our strident individualism. We had to make some tough choices. One choice was to move back into the neighborhood *as a congregation*.

In my third year, I preached a sermon on Jeremiah 29, wherein Jeremiah writes a letter to those exiled in Babylon, instructing them to "build houses and live in them, plant gardens and eat what they produce, take wives and have sons and daughters, seek the peace of the city and

---

31. Quoted in Wolter, *Principles of Monasticism*, 43.

32. I will return to this theme in the final chapter and develop it further.

pray for it."[33] I told the congregation that I believed that we were not here by accident and set out a challenge for some in the congregation to move back into Grandview-Woodlands and to commit to the neighborhood's well being for the long haul like those exiles. It was one of the few sermons where some people came right out and told me they disagreed with it, an uncommon experience in a "polite" Canadian church. Yet that vision planted a seed that germinated with the beginnings of Salsbury Community Society,[34] and it was through the establishment of this society that the practice of living in community and welcoming others became part of the fabric of the church.

Salsbury's beginnings appeared to be short-lived. A group formed initially with the intent to develop a community offering affordable housing in a senior's home five blocks from the church. Zoning restrictions on the change of use for the building, however, made the project financially unviable. Despondent over the news, many in the group were convinced that the dream of forming this community was dead. But then a veteran in community living among us suggested we simply search for houses in close proximity, where people could share a common life. When someone else named the two houses adjacent to the church, a new dream was birthed, one for a house where "refugee claimants, seniors, single parents . . ." could come "to live together, offering and receiving each others' gifts— not as participants in a program, but rather housemates . . . intentional about participating in each others' lives."[35]

The establishment of these houses thrust us to root in the Grandview-Woodlands neighborhood even further as we began to model a way of life together that many people would be drawn into and others would seek to imitate. In these houses, people chose to live together for varying reasons such as economic need, loneliness, support to overcome addictions, help in the struggle with mental illness or support for adapting to a new country. Whatever the need, to live in one of these houses committed the people to a shared life around a common kitchen and living room. While

33. Jer 29:5–7, paraphrased. Ray Bakke's influence here is evident. See Bakke, *Theology as Big as the City*.

34. The sermon was retrieved on February 5, 2008, from http://salsburycommunity society.com.

35. Retrieved February 15, 2008, from http://salsbury.community.society.com.

there was a core of people in each house who held that vision of community, each person in the house was challenged to share in this common life around meals and everyday conversation.

Kinbrace House, named by combining the words "kinship" and "embrace," was specifically dedicated to providing short-term housing for refugee claimants, one of the most vulnerable groups in society. During stays that varied from one month to a year, folks from around the globe were accompanied to banks, stores, government offices and refugee hearings. The welcome these refugee claimants received countered the hostility they faced elsewhere.

> When I am outside in the city, I am afraid to tell people I am a refugee claimant, even though I am legally allowed to be one, because I feel shunned, as though I am a danger to society. At my new home I feel like I am known for who I am, as a person who has a history and a future.[36]

While the "core" folk in these houses are part of GCBC, most of the newcomers in the Salsbury Community Society houses are not, though many have become part of the church, and some have converted to Christ and been baptized along the way. In these houses, the gospel is "overheard" in the lives of those seeking to follow Christ. People have the opportunity to see for themselves the shape of a gospel-formed life and are welcomed naturally into practices of prayer, forgiveness, hospitality and service.

> I didn't know [the people at Kinbrace House] and I was a stranger and they gave me a place to stay. And I realized that this was more than a place because they were interested in having relationships with me and talking and having food and stories.

From Kinbrace House, this refugee was enfolded into the life of the larger community and then integrated into Emmaus House, one of the other houses in the Salsbury Community Society.

> The time I spent in Emmaus house . . . was very significant because I became one of the community. It was not only . . . managing to live together; it was an openness to one another. I was part of the fabric of the house. My point of view was welcomed . . . They wanted to

---

36. The entire interview can be found in *Cohere*, 4. Cohere is the Salsbury Community Society newsletter.

> *integrate me into the family . . . Emmaus was an expression of the*
> *church.*

In a culture of "marketing," where the gospel can easily metamorphose into another commodity for self-seeking consumers, living in community and sharing a home together exposes people to the joys and struggles of an authentic Christian life, opening them to the possibilities of a new *way of living* in Christ, which they can explore and try out for themselves.[37]

> *I came into this faith community not feeling isolated from other*
> *people but having isolated circles of networks and relationships, so*
> *it was very much consumer driven . . . My challenge and growth has*
> *been to locate in this neighborhood, in which is the church, what*
> *has now over years become the realm of family. And then the radi-*
> *cal hospitality piece is being challenged through living in one of the*
> *homes and having regular contact with people who are either very*
> *different from me or in places of vulnerability.*

I am not suggesting that community living is some sort of magic answer to the renewal of the church in North America. But I do believe that when people seek to share life together around a common vision and practices of the kingdom of God, they are swept into the vortex of transforming power, both for themselves and those who are welcomed into their small community. As we let the possibility of sharing our homes with others seep into our imaginations, we resist the trend in our culture to designate our houses as private spaces, designed to exclude others except when we invite them to cross our treasured thresholds. Whether we choose to live in community or not, every one of us must figure out how to shape our lives so that they can be shared to a significant degree with others, though this is difficult when the prevailing trend in our culture is to organize our lives based on maximum personal benefit. To live the gospel apart from a shared life of hospitality is a woefully inadequate expression of the gospel vision. As Krister Stendahl remarks, "wherever, whenever, however the kingdom manifests itself, it is welcome."[38] There

37. See Guder, *Continuing Conversion of the Church* for a description of the church's cultural captivity along these lines.

38. As quoted in Pohl, *Making Room*, 8.

is a reason Christ followers keep looking back to those early days of the church for inspiration.

At the early stages of our experiments in community living, we felt like teenagers learning to dance. We were awkward, quick to stumble and often felt like bolting for the door. Living with others, particularly with those whom you are seeking to build a shared life, inevitably exposes your vices. That was certainly our experience when our family began sharing our home in 1991, two years after we had moved to the neighborhood. When the church purchased the house next door, we moved in, and one year later, we leased the ground floor to a student couple from Ecuador who were given a stipend by the church to assist us in building relationships among Central American refugees. When they moved elsewhere, we welcomed a single woman recovering from a divorce and depression, then a single mother and her little boy, who was in the same age range as our three young sons.

At each step, we integrated our lives with our housemates more, first renting the basement, then sharing the house with someone who spent most of her time in her room, finally sharing the entire house with a family. With each increasing step in our shared use of space and overlapping lives, we experienced the "normal" development of relationships: an appreciation of the other person's gifts in the first couple of months, followed by a growing annoyance with certain habits of our housemates (which they developed with us, too). In our third experience of sharing our home, we worked through the most conflict, as we argued about parenting styles, childcare and household responsibilities. We faced a pivotal decision: Would we persevere and seek to resolve these problems, or would we ask the person to leave and quit this shared life? Choosing to persevere with more than thirty people who have lived with us over the last sixteen years has led us into what Bernard of Clairvaux calls "the school of love."[39]

What we came to realize, along with many others in our neighborhood who were sharing their homes, was that the ideals of community—friendship, economic and emotional support, love—come with a cost. They require us to let go of our cherished and exalted views of our own moral goodness and face one another with our naked personas.[40] Jean

39. See Pennington, *School of Love*, 4.

40. For a description of this transformational process which community living elicits,

Vanier, the founder of L'Arche communities, says that, "in order to accept other people's disabilities and to help them grow, it was fundamental for me to accept my own. I have after all, learned something of my own character."[41]

In my interviews of people in our church, many have described this "stripping away" of our impatience, selfishness, greed (and a host of other vices) by living in community. One woman describes her experience of this process not only with the people she lives with but with the many people who live in proximity to one another as part of the church:

> *I have been challenged too because our lives overlap in so many areas, not everyone in the church, but many of us. So I have been challenged to learn how to grow in being community for the long haul. So often in North America, our lives are compartmentalized, but here our lives really overlap. So I am forced to let people see parts of me that are not very nice and I see that of other people. And so [we encounter] the challenge of learning how to live together well, when so much of our lives are interconnected.*

Another identified that she learned what *"everyone living in community learns . . . It is stretching. It requires you to think clearly about things and learn to communicate."* Another person who has sixteen years experience of living in community put it this way: "[*Community living*] *is also a mirror of finally seeing who I really am and then noticing that same thing in another person, so we become brother and sister rather than our perceptions being separate.*"

The challenge of the corporate Christian life—a challenge we often fail to prepare others for when we invite them into community—is to realize that shared life inevitably exposes both our character blemishes and shortcomings as well as our need to turn to God and discover the Spirit's power for change. The apostle Paul regularly instructs the churches to view community life in Christ as the context whereby God does this work of transformation in them (cf. Col 3:1–16). As Christine Pohl confirms, community living forces you to face your own faults:

---

see Vanier, *Community and Growth*, 104–64. The entire book reads like a manual of what to expect and what is required when living with others.

41. Vanier, *Becoming Human*, 101.

> A life of hospitality means a more continual interaction with oth-
> ers, and fewer opportunities to carefully project a "perfect image"
> .... To try to hide weaknesses within a community would be very
> pompous. To be so uptight and try to put on a show for eighteen
> hours a day is unworkable. No one can last long in a community
> of hospitality without acknowledging weakness and frailty. We
> can't share all of our life "except for our failures."[42]

One person in our church compares this transforming process to the similar path in marriage: "*Certainly, in marriage, but obviously in the context of living closely with others . . . it was quite transformative to shift . . . from seeing people's limitations as a hindrance and a liability to seeing them as stirring up a place of creativity which goodness can come from.*"

This same process of developing more honest, transforming relationships was transpiring in our church home groups as well. Since the amount of interaction in a home group is much more controlled than in a community house, the process described above may take longer. However, over time, these contexts can foster relationships of honesty that lead to transformation as well. Indeed, a group that does not traverse through a stage of conflict and communicate more transparently rarely progresses to a stage of cohesive mission and purpose.[43] When people gather together in the presence of God to pattern their lives after the life of Christ, when they interact with scripture, when they practice prayer and love each other, they, too, are exposed to the obstacles to implementing this vision of community and become aware of their need for God.

My own home group, one of seven we had developed by our seventh year with the church, profoundly experienced this transformation. One member in particular dominated our group discussions, occasionally berated others and often frustrated members by swaying all conversation towards his own interests or struggles. These responses were exacerbated by his manic depression. One night, in the middle of our evening, he left with an outburst. When he returned an hour later, we took the rest of the evening to express our pent-up frustrations with his domination, offered forgiveness, moved deeper to discuss his feelings of alienation and self-judgment, and spoke words of affirmation, affection and commitment.

42. Pohl, *Making Room*, 118.

43. Sofield et al., *Building Community*, 23.

The next week, the man returned to say with gratitude, "*If I'd had all of you in my life twenty years ago, I wouldn't have gotten into so much trouble.*" After this turning point in his sense of belonging to the group and the church, his gifts emerged: he could detect emotional pain in others and step towards these persons with appropriate physical touch and emotional empathy. For the members of our home group, the experience on that night tutored all of us in the power of forgiveness, love and acceptance. Experiences like these in our home groups and our community houses have given us all courage to embrace rather than run from community.

Part of what we were learning is that long-term relationships, particularly when you are seeking to accomplish goals and work towards change, inevitably get messy. One person who has been part of the church for ten years reflects:

> *I have never lived one place as long as I have lived here. So then you are in relationships and you have got to live with those relationships and find ways through difficult issues and confrontations, personalities that don't jive with my own personality. So I think this is what has been the challenge. I think probably my own instinct is to just head off in another direction—that is the pattern in my life—not running away from things, but you can always just change course a bit—but here you have to address it, you have to move through those things, there has not been a lot of confrontation or difficulty but I think that when there has been, there has been a mature way of going through it or a maturing way for me.*

In a culture where many relational bonds resemble "liquid love," learning to love one another through time and struggle can bear witness to God's covenant love.[44]

Having these community homes at the core of our church's vision and practice has widened the imagination of those who have joined our church more recently. Seeing what this shared life looks like—whether that is described during our worship or discovered as people participate in home groups or as people share meals as guests in one of these homes— offers people a non-threatening opportunity to explore living differently. That slow exposure gradually removes some of the fear related to our need for privacy and protection. As such, this modeling moves the radi-

44. Bauman, *Liquid Love*, 73–91.

cal closer to the ordinary. One person, who never thought she would be sharing a home with "non-family" members, remarks: *"[I'm] finding that people who are not necessarily radical are wanting to live [with others] in an apartment or house in a nuclear family situation . . . I would have never expected that of me."*

Over the years, the core of our church has exhibited a growing desire to share life in more deliberate and intentional ways, believing that community, demanding as it can be, is basic to the gospel:

> *I have seen more and more people moving into and looking for ways of being in some type of intentional community, whether it is actually living in the house together or living locally or people grappling with [how] they could locate near each other . . . I really see a movement of . . . more and more people . . . saying that they want to move from isolation.*

Though the demands of community are stretching, there is a growing recognition that this stretching is for our good.

Perhaps a root question that we need to ask one another as Christ-followers is whether we still believe that we are *all* flawed and in need of reshaping into the image of God. If we are, then we best admit it and expect that being the church together will scream out our need for personal change.

THREE

Navigating the Rapids of Privacy, Possessions, and Power

There he was, homeless. Would a church take Him in today—feed Him, clothe Him, offer Him a bed? I hope I ask myself that question on the last day of my life. I once prayed and prayed to God that He never, ever let me forget to ask that question.[1]

In popular culture, hospitality often implies sending invitations to a predetermined group of suave guests, decorating our houses according to Martha Stewart's latest tips and serving a perfectly planned gourmet feast. The roots of this word, however, go back to the early Christian practice of welcoming the stranger and the poor—as well as the wealthy—into a shared life and mission.[2] This welcome of the stranger is rooted in God's welcome towards us "while we were yet sinners."[3] God's welcome to the stranger runs like a thread throughout Scripture, from the gathering and deliverance of the Hebrew people in the Exodus, to Jesus' hosting of meals for those who were unlikely guests,[4] to the practice of hospitality to the stranger by the Body of Christ, the church.[5]

---

1. Dorothy Day, quoted from an interview with Robert Coles in Pohl, *Making Room*, 96.

2. See Pohl, *Making Room*, 17.

3. Rom 5:8.

4. E.g., Luke 9:12–17; 18:15–17.

5. E.g., Rom 12:8; Heb 13:2.

Extending God's Welcome Through Radical Hospitality

Several biblical texts have inspired and influenced our church to embrace the practice of radical hospitality. The words of Jesus, "whoever welcomes the least of these welcomes me,"[6] single out the naked, the hungry, the sick, and the stranger as those to whom Jesus' followers should extend hospitality. A similar group is in view in Jesus' parable of the banquet:

> When you give a luncheon or dinner, do not invite your friends or brothers or your relatives or rich neighbours, in case they may invite you in return, and you would be repaid. But when you give a banquet, invite the poor, the crippled, the lame and the blind. And you will be blessed, because they cannot repay you, for you will be repaid at the resurrection of the righteous.[7]

Extending God's Welcome at the Table

One way our church has sought to live out this movement towards radical hospitality has been through the rhythm of hosting a weekly dinner for our friends who live on or near the streets. All who have participated in this weekly meal over the past eleven years have encountered the basic contours of a God-shaped hospitality, where "the distinctive quality . . . is that it offers a generous welcome to the least, without concern for advantage or benefit to the host. Such hospitality reflects God's greater hospitality that welcomes the undeserving, provides the lonely with a home, and sets a banquet table for the hungry."[8]

The weekly practice of hosting this meal began with two women in our congregation who felt stirred to prepare Christmas dinners for the host of folks from our neighborhood who either lived on the street or were running out of money and food before the end of the month. Around the same time, while attending a Grandview-Woodlands Area Services team meeting, a neighborhood advocate for mental health patients asked me what the churches were doing for the increasing number of people on the street along Commercial Drive. My response was revealing: *"Nothing."*

6. Matt 25:40.

7. Luke 14:12–14.

8. Pohl, *Making Room*, 16.

But I asked our congregation that question in my sermon on Sunday and invited anyone interested in exploring a response to meet after the service. About fifteen people came for a discussion, and after researching responses in other cities, a group submitted a proposal for "Out of the Cold" to the church council. After the congregation talked through concerns about damage to the church building and affordability, we began in the fall with about sixty guests per week on average in the first six months. Later, the program was expanded to include an overnight stay, with breakfast the following morning, during the colder six months of the year.

Those involved with Out of the Cold have thought carefully about how to create an environment that blurs the lines between volunteers and guests. As volunteers and guests arrive, some mingle, some read the paper, some play games, some help with set up and others prepare the meal. Rather than creating a program that is all about filling the stomachs of the "needy," volunteers and guests eat together, which reduces fear and suspicion while fostering mutuality. As volunteers converse with individuals with whom they might not normally share the table, they learn each other's names and enjoy a quality meal together.[9] When they leave the meal, both are prepared to greet each other if and when they meet in the street. After the meal, some clean up, some watch a movie, some receive prayer, some get hair cuts, and others gather together for a Bible study. All in all, the night has less the feel of a "feeding line" and more the tenor of a community of people gathering to share an evening together.[10] *"The years that I was involved, I got to know people who I still know on the Drive. [Participating in Out of the Cold] moved me into a relational space that I am very grateful for."*

This welcoming environment also challenged everyone involved to reflect on our own attitudes and responses towards the guests. Many of us were drawn towards this type of hospitality because we had a desire to "fix" a problem—and then discovered that the transformation being

---

9. As one chef said, "We serve what we'd make for guests in our home." There is always a vegetarian option as well, which has been important for those who have made a choice to reduce or exclude meat from their diet.

10. As more people are now living in poverty and the numbers at the meal have grown—with some guests arriving drunk—it has become difficult to foster this community environment. At the same time, there have been remarkably few incidences of violence, and guests often admonish other guests who are making others uncomfortable.

called for, first and foremost, was within ourselves. Each of us faced different but penetrating questions: Why are we afraid of these folk? Why do we feel the need to "fix" others? Why do we assume that all poverty is primarily the individual's fault? Why does it feel freeing to be among people who lack status in society or who have no hope of gaining power? Why is this meal so celebrative and rooting for me, even though talking to people can be so tough some nights?[11]

Many of our volunteers and core staff have had to shift their orientation from the posture of "giver" or "the healthy one" to one of mutual engagement as humans created in God's image, valued by God and in need of redemption. Miroslav Volf identifies this stance of mutuality in relationship as "the will to give ourselves to others and welcome them, to readjust our identities to make space for them . . . prior to any judgement about others, except to identifying them in their humanity."[12] Sharing the table at Out of the Cold calls both middle-class volunteers and people on or near the street to cross socially constructed boundaries in their own spheres, develop new circles of relationships and move towards mutual transformation. This forces all involved to resist the "*tendency*," as one volunteer shared, "*to pull back into what is known or familiar or develop friendship with people who are like you and spend relational energy there.*"

 One of the benefits of "institutional spaces" like Out of the Cold is that they create a safe, public place for initial encounters among strangers where trust can be established. Often, "hospitality begins at the gate, in the doorway, on the bridges, between public and private spaces."[13] We need places like this in society where fears of danger and deception can be overcome so that people can then move deeper into friendship. The challenge for all of us is to resist the temptation to become comfortable in this place, self-satisfied with our "good work," and so get stalled at this level without ever welcoming these strangers-turned-friends deeper into our lives.

11. These are all questions that volunteers posed to me or that I confronted myself.

12. Volf, *Exclusion and Embrace*, 29.

13. Pohl, *Making Room*, 95.

Extending God's Welcome into Our Homes

In order to move beyond this initial welcome of the stranger within the safety of institutional places, we will need to open ourselves to encounters with our new friends during unscheduled and inconvenient moments, and from there extend our welcome over the secured boundaries of the place we call "home." Speaking of our tendency to construct very highly controlled boundaries around our places of residence, Bouma-Prediger and Walsh remark:

> Boundaries used to erect forces of self-protection, then, can never be refuges of hospitality. The walls are simply too thick, the barriers too impenetrable. But boundaries that demarcate and define spaces and identities need not be exclusionary . . . Boundaries can be horizons that provide a sense of orientation, yet are dynamic. Boundaries are not there so much to stop something from coming in (though, that remains part of the safety-producing function of boundaries) as they are to provide a context for a certain kind of unfolding or opening up that happens within those boundaries.[14]

This movement towards opening up our lives and homes, which had begun in our attempts to live more communally and through Out of the Cold, expanded even more in 2000, when the church rented a house around the corner as a space where guests from Out of the Cold and those on the street could gather in the living room, or "the waiting room," as one of our staff used to call it.[15] The activities in this house, along with street outreach connected with it, became known as Crossroads Community Project. Once in the house, guests could use one of the computers, join others in the art room, gather clothing from the wardrobe, take a shower, do some laundry, see a counsellor, participate in a discussion group or just rest out of the rain. The house provided a step towards deeper and more intimate relationships between guests and volunteers (and among guests themselves).

However, after unsuccessfully trying to purchase that house and then trying to move Crossroads into one of the houses adjacent to the church

---

14. Bouma-Prediger and Walsh, *Beyond Homelessness*, 53–54.

15. Our outreach worker wrote an entire description of how the house functions based on this waiting-room model, where people could choose to move from the living room to another room when they were ready.

building, we ended up closing the Crossroads house four years later, questioning whether this "house with social services" was the best model for community development. In a proposal entitled "Phoenix from amidst the ashes," one of our advisory committee proposed that we shift instead to a model of moving out to where our friends were and welcoming them further into our own lives. This vision called for us to connect people with resources already existing on the Drive and to welcome those neighbors who had first frequented Out of the Cold and then the Crossroads house into our own homes, a further step in our move along this trajectory towards radical hospitality.

Two couples in particular embodied this vision and stirred the imagination of others in our congregation—and in the neighborhood—towards a more radical hospitality when they intentionally moved into a duplex five blocks from the church building and began welcoming their friends from Out of the Cold, Crossroads and the streets of the neighborhood into their home. Both couples had already had experience living in Salsbury Community houses and had also developed numerous, quality relationships with people from Out of the Cold and Crossroads. One of the couples describes how their house operates:

> We would like to say that it functions as a place of occasional and temporary refuge for people who don't have a place and who live on the street mostly or who live in places of isolation. It provides a place for some basic resources. To have a shower, or use the laundry or phone or the internet or whatever. It also provides a bit of a refuge from the street so if you want to not just come in and get warm and dry but also just want to be in a safe place where they can sit and watch TV or something or watch a movie. We also have open meals five or six times a week, so people can come and join us for that. So it provides a space that is actually shared by all of us . . . often enough, people that come from the neighborhood and hang out at our place are there more than we are so a number of them know their way around the place and just hunker down. A few people we know have been on the street and aren't feeling well, so we will say to them—"do you want a couple of days, like do you want a little respite?"

This family went from welcoming students, to welcoming more vulnerable people to live with them as part of a community, to this deeper embrace of their friends on the street. The progression towards this way of life did not happen overnight, but was a trajectory pursued over the last twelve years:

> *From living on our own as a family, at first having people live with us mostly to just help with the rent, and then because of our involvement with other things, seeing a real gap in the community's ability to provide housing for people. From there we began thinking about how we might not necessarily provide housing for a student but [for someone] who might not be able to find it, who might have difficulty getting good secure housing and housing that had a component of being a part of a quasi-healthy family. So to give someone a sense of family who didn't have that, I think that was a good thing.*

Jimmy Dorrell, co-founder of Mission Waco in Texas, describes this incremental movement towards deeper and more radical hospitality:

> Like most spiritual discipleship, movement toward hospitality to the stranger comes through baby steps, through consistent and growing acts of kindness in guided institutional settings. Before we invite the homeless man into our home, we can visit the local soup kitchen or shelter to gain a new level of comfort among people who may come from a completely different background. We can volunteer at the food bank, lead a Bible study at an alcohol and drug treatment faculty, mentor the child of an incarcerated parent, or tutor a young person in juvenile detention. With each visit, familiarity overcomes formerly imagined fears; we begin to notice our commonalities instead of our differences. With new confidence and call, we are much more prepared to open our homes, share our possessions, and overlook the differences that divide us. Like Jesus' initiative with Zacchaeus, we can boldly go into settings that were formerly uncomfortable to us and where others disapprove.[16]

Our own experience reflects this truth: as we have welcomed housemates, these housemates and our children themselves have often become the primary hosts to welcome others in the neighborhood, taking the lead when we are tired or busy.

Other households in our neighborhood have not taken the same shape as the house described above, but they have taken steps toward

---

16. Dorrell, "Pass the Potatoes, Please," 73.

more multifaceted relationships with friends on the street, welcoming them in for meals, coffee, conversation, or a place to sleep. After observing how many of the people who lived for a transitional period in the Salsbury Community houses still could not find secure housing after they moved out, one house decided to live longer-term with those who were present, but to welcome others to shared meals and for shorter overnight stays in a designated guest room.

Providing this transitional housing is a long-standing Christian tradition. In the fourth century, Chrysostom urged his parishioners to make a guest chamber in their own homes, a place set apart for Christ—a place within which to welcome "the maimed, the beggars and the homeless."[17] Recognizing that some Christians would hesitate to take strangers into their homes or guest rooms, Chrysostom suggested that they could at least make a place in their household for a local poor person who was known to them. One wonders how this practice could dramatically alleviate homelessness in our cities. Perhaps the greater problem in our urban centers is not homelessness, but rather too many empty bedrooms.

While a single person, a nuclear family, or even a typical local church alone would find this radical hospitality overwhelming, the established network of relationships in a community can provide the additional support and energy necessary to make this welcome possible. When one person in a community house is occupied or fatigued, for example, another can be present to engage a particularly needy guest. Over the past eighteen years, we have discovered as a church that recovering the practice of hospitality to strangers over the long haul requires a community to share the burdens and the risks.

> I think when we talk about radical hospitality, where I see us getting into trouble is when we try and do it in isolation. Speaking for myself, that is when we have run into trouble. Yet the times that it has worked for me are the times that it has happened within community. Which means to some extent that you don't have the glory of the monk in Les Mis, but you share it among the people and it goes really well.

Like other "new monastic" communities across North America, living together and extending hospitality has impacted our congregation's

17. Chrysostom, "Homily 45," 277.

view of possessions and privacy.[18] As people have shared homes, they have also begun to share tools, food and even the "sacred" car with non-family members. Reminiscent of Luke's description of the early church in the first part of Acts, there is a growing attempt to give to everyone "as he had need."[19]

Our own experience as a family has been that sharing our home and possessions has brought us a greater degree of freedom, especially from the necessity to protect and guard ourselves, allowing for a deepening trust in others. As Christine Pohl observes, "Hospitable attitudes, even a principled commitment to hospitality, do not challenge us or transform our loyalties in the way that actual hospitality to particular strangers does. Hospitality in the abstract lacks the mundane, troublesome yet rich dimensions of a profound human practice."[20] We have been delighted as parents to see our boys learn to carry the conversation with a stranger who joins us at the dinner table, interacting with our guests with a freedom borne from years of observing and taking up this practice of hospitality themselves. The Hebrew notion of living with an open hand instead of tight fisted certainly has lead us into joy.[21]

Radical Hospitality as a Way of Life

Ron, who journeyed with our church community for more than fifteen years, struggled with mental illness most of his life. Awkward in conversation, he was quick to tell complete strangers the story of losing his family in a fire at the age of five. Ron eventually found a room right across from the church building, and for several years, he made his way around the neighborhood, stopping to ask people if he could pray for them, or joining them for a meal. When one of his closest friends in the neighborhood hosted a birthday party for him, he was ecstatic and thanked everyone

18. See Claiborne, "Sharing Economic Resources," 26–38. For a more detailed description of Shane's own biography and the community he began, see *Irresistible Revolution,* and their website at http://thesimpleway.org.

19. Acts 4:35.

20. Pohl, *Making Room*, 14.

21. See Deut 15:7–8. "If there is a poor person among your brothers and sisters in any of the towns of the land that the Lord your God is giving you, do not be hardhearted or tight fisted toward your brother or sister. Rather be open handed."

who came, testifying that this had been his first birthday party in over thirty years. In his increasingly non-threatening and attentive way with both men and women, Ron began to offer words of encouragement and exhortation to each of us, often telling us how much God cared for us.

When Ron died a few years ago, those of us who knew him realized that he had become like a chaplain to our community. The words in Heb 13:1–2 spoke of our life with him: "*Let love of the brothers and sisters continue. Do not neglect to show hospitality to strangers, for by this some have entertained angels without knowing it.*"

Telling stories like Ron's is important, because they help those who are new to the church witness how radical hospitality unleashes the healing power of God. Two couples in our congregation recently bought a house together for both economic and lifestyle reasons: they want to live a more hospitable life. When I interviewed them in our worship service, M. said that six years ago, when they first joined the church, they thought people who lived together apart from family bonds were nuts. But watching, participating and dialoguing with others who are pursuing this way of life has attracted her to a life shared with others in community. Apart from this hands-on opportunity, this individual—and others like her—would not have been able to overcome her fears.

One of the unique features of GCBC, in contrast to many of the new monastic communities, is that this move towards community and radical hospitality lies at the core of the church's vision and practice.[22] In both our worship and community events, this vision of receiving and extending the welcome of God is celebrated and affirmed.[23] As people in our congregation witness others living in community, opening up their homes, sharing possessions, and extending the radical welcome of Christ to others, they come to see that radical hospitality "*means a giving up of our 'rights' in order to move into hospitality . . . not as charity but actually because it is the way of life.*"

22. Many of the new monastic communities lie on the periphery of the church, although they seek to contribute to its renewal rather than rejecting the church, as renewal groups are prone to do. See Kauffman, "Humble Submission to Christ's Body," 68–79.

23. The church has grown in size to around three hundred people, counting members from our two worshipping communities, and many of the people who have been welcomed into our congregation, programs and homes are witnessing this way of life for the first time—at first passively, then in more participative ways.

Sustaining a Life of Radical Hospitality

Recently, someone was asked to stay away from Out of the Cold and the Salsbury Community houses because his behavior when intoxicated was violent and harmful to others. Following Jesus' teaching in Matt 18:15–20, we tried to confront this person with love, but it was challenging and even frightening for some of those present. "*People come with lots of issues around violence or addictions . . . that can . . . [disturb] the safety or the serenity of the place.*" One man who lost his sobriety after a five month rehabilitation has become harder and more violent, physically harming a few of the people who help at our community meal in his drunken anger.

When people don't appreciate our welcome, it can be demoralizing, too.

> *I tried it. I had a 14 year old kid literally from the street into our house and I gave her all my patience and all my might to try to change her, and it could not be done. I wonder, where are the limits? How radical can we be?*

> ***

> *I think one of the things [for me] is fighting occasionally with feelings of being taken advantage of. The sense of taking, taking, taking.*

 We have also had to wrestle with questions about how to live hospitably with young children and how to sustain our commitment to radical hospitality as a way of life.

> *I see an obstacle . . . from my own perspective [in] figuring out what [radical hospitality] looks like practically speaking with a family of three small kids. Does that mean we have homeless people sleeping in our front entry way?*

> ***

> *I think we need to wrestle with the very real questions that come with radical hospitality . . . Some of these questions can be barriers, because people don't know how to push past them . . . What kind of spirituality sustains radical hospitality? Because many people are also feeling on the edge of burnout so we need a way of pushing into that so it gives life to all, everyone.*

As we have embraced radical hospitality as a practice within our congregation, we have had to wrestle with many demanding questions. What does it mean to love our neighbor as ourselves when the culture around us is becoming more isolated and focused on protecting what is "ours"? Since neglect and abandonment have wounded so many of the "strangers" we're trying to welcome into our hearts and homes, how can we gain our friends' trust and empower them to face barriers to growth and move toward healing? How can we be truly loving and not just tolerant? How can we be freed from cultural notions of nicety and embrace biblical notions of sacrificial, covenant compassion? But as we continue to work through these challenges together, we are led deeper and further into God's transformational mission—seeing signs of transformation within ourselves, our church and our neighborhood.

Worship as Welcome

In this move toward community and radical hospitality, we have begun to view our worship as the central way in which we as a community are corporately welcomed by God in Christ through the Spirit. Elizabeth Newman explains how worship itself is an act of hospitality: "To sing, to pray, to pass the peace, to listen to God's word, to eat at God's table is to share through the gift and power of the Spirit, in God's own giving and receiving. Such a vision of worship . . . enables us to practice hospitality more faithfully."[24]

Over the years, I have witnessed our congregation shift away from trying to create a "rousing worship service" that would attract people towards seeing worship as a way of responding to God's welcome so that we can be (re)formed as the people of God and sent out to share in God's mission for the world. Those responses include praise/adoration/thanksgiving, performing the Scriptures (often dramatically acting out narrative portions), lament, confession, intercession, listening to each other and to the world around us, hearing the word preached, gathering around the table and being sent out into mission.[25] By reading Scripture, singing and

24. Newman, *Untamed Hospitality*, 42.

25. Some of these may receive greater focus at specific times of the year e.g. lament during Lent. For a description of the practices that form us as the people of God, see Wilson, *Why Church Matters*.

praying in our congregant's first languages, as well as including art from the many cultures represented in our international church, we have widened the welcome even more.

Shaping our worship around the liturgical seasons of the church year (Advent, Christmas, Epiphany, Lent, Easter, Pentecost and ordinary time) has connected our body to the worship and life of the universal church. The seasons of the church awaken us to the narrative and actions of God in our history and our present, reshaping, re-enchanting and re-sacralizing what Charles Taylor describes as the "empty, homogenous time" of our modern (and postmodern) world.[26] The practice of creating art and hanging it in our sanctuary for each of these seasons, especially the creative renditions of the stations of the cross made and hung each Lent, has heightened our senses and experience of this narrative, integrating the visual with the auditory in our worship of God. By gathering each week for worship, we as a community are welcomed back to God and to one another so that we might extend that radical welcome of God in Christ to our neighbors and the whole world.

When people ask me what they can do to help their church become more radically hospitable, I try to encourage them first to become more hospitable themselves so that their life can be observed by others and spark the imagination of their community.

God's Welcome in the Eucharist

The central act by which we are welcomed by God in Christ during our communal worship is through communion, the Eucharist, or the Lord's Supper. Jonathan Wilson reflects on how this meal shapes us: "The Lord's Supper incorporates us into the life of the kingdom by the act of remembering Christ as the One who teaches and embodies the kingdom."[27] Over the last two decades, our practice of celebrating the Lord's Supper has also changed, moving from passing the bread and cup around the pews to gathering in groups around tables where we could pray for each other, or processing forward to share in a common loaf and cup. When we began our second "evening" congregation four years ago, we made the Eucharist

26. Taylor, *Secular Age*, 54–59.
27. Wilson, *Why Church Matters*, 109.

the centerpiece of our worship, celebrating it weekly (in contrast to once each month in our morning worship) and offering prayer as people come forward. This practice has influenced our morning congregation to celebrate the Lord's Supper more regularly, in recognition of how this act forms us according to the pattern of the death and resurrection of Jesus.[28] Only by receiving God's welcome in the Eucharist with each other can we begin the movement towards welcoming others, which leads us down the road towards integrated multicultural life and seeking justice for others.

Celebrating the meal Jesus gave us has led naturally into sharing meals together following our worship, a practice which both our congregations have valued. By sharing in meals together, rich and poor, immigrant and native, male and female, "educated" and life-taught, we extend this welcome from God to one another. Sharing meals has been integral to nearly all of our programs, all of our community houses and both our congregations, and for good reason: "A shared meal is the activity most closely tied to the reality of God's Kingdom, just as it is the most basic expression of hospitality."[29] By eating together, we receive the gifts of God—food, taste, sustenance, conversation and care—and extend those gifts to each other. By eating together, we receive and extend the welcome of God, moving from isolation to community, and then extend that welcome to the neighborhood. In following this trajectory, we move from self to others, a movement which re-awakens us to our common need for the grace and mercy of Christ, completing the circle of life in Christ

I believe that this movement from isolation to community towards radical hospitality is essential to the future of our church and the church as a whole. Jean Vanier suggests that the church's venture into radical hospitality will be essential for the future of our society:

> In years to come, we are going to need many small communities which will welcome lost and lonely people, offering them a new form of family and a sense of belonging. In the past, Christians who wanted to follow Jesus opened hospitals and schools. Now that there are many of these, Christians must commit themselves to these new communities of welcome, to live with people who

28. Notice Paul's description of the Christian life according to this pattern in Philippians 3.

29. Pohl, *Making Room*, 30.

have no other family and to show them that they are loved and can grow to greater freedom and that they, in turn, can love and give life to others.[30]

Our story thus far suggests that his words are prophetic and true. Could it be that God is raising up these types of communities in every corner of our cities for this very purpose? Could it be that these communities will be tributaries leading us back to the life-giving river that flows from the gospel?

30. Vanier, *Community and Growth*, 283.

FOUR

Navigating the Rapids of Complacency and Religious Consumerism

Do we first accept Christian beliefs and then engage in Christian practices, or is it the other way around?[1]

In an age of religious consumerism, where so many people either become dissatisfied with the church and quit, or drift to larger churches that can offer better religious "goods," the focus on common practices shifts our understanding of the church away from an institutional service provider towards a movement. By taking up common practices that are shaped by the gospel, the church becomes a community of diverse people seeking to take up a more deeply integrated life that unites belief and action. In this latter understanding, the purpose of the church is not to get more people into the church building, but to invite people to participate in the mission of God in the world, a mission that brings restoration, renewal and hope to our neighbors, city and world.

Craig Dykstra and Dorothy Bass define Christian practices as "things Christian people do together over time to address fundamental human needs in response to and in the light of God's active presence for the life of the world," and they identify four reasons that the terminology of "practices" is fruitful for Christianity.[2] First, practices resist the separation

1. Volf, "Theology for a Way of Life," 255–56.
2. Dykstra and Bass, "Theological Understanding of Christian Practices," 18.

of thinking from action, and thus of Christian doctrine from Christian life, thereby bridging the unhealthy dualism which characterizes so many branches of the church. Second, practices are social, belonging to groups of people across generations—a feature that undergirds the communal quality of the Christian life. Third, practices are rooted in the past but are also constantly adaptive to changing circumstances, including new cultural settings. Fourth, practices articulate wisdom that is in the keeping of practitioners who do not always think of themselves as theologians, thus engaging the wider church in theological reflection.[3]

Evangelically rooted churches can so easily slip into forming biblically literate people and stop there, rather than forming disciples of Christ. But Jesus taught us to live as salt, light and leaven in our world, and he was openly critical of those for whom belief was merely a cognitive idea that did not coincide with transformed living. Practices shape the people of a church into a community of mission, restoring vitality and hope both to its members and its neighborhood.

GUIDING A COMMUNITY TOWARDS SHARED PRACTICES

> The key pathology of our time, which seduces us all, is the reduction of the imagination so that we are too numbed, satiated and co-opted to do serious imaginative work.[4]

One of the catalysts towards renewal for our community was our re-visioning process. By gathering weekly in homes for a month to talk about our church's vision, the people of the congregation moved out of the sanctuary and forged new relationships within the intimate space of the home. That process also began to rebuild the congregation's decision-making muscle, as most of the fifty or so adults who were part of the church participated in this process.[5] By slowly forming a shared vision with common goals for the future, the congregation began to realize that we still held a capacity for corporate action, an ability that seemed to have waned over the previous decade. Furthermore, by naming our unified intention to

3. Bass, "Introduction," 6.

4. Brueggemann, *Interpretation and Obedience*, 199.

5. Bakke articulates the importance of renewing this capacity, especially in the early stages of urban church renewal. See Bakke, *Urban Christian*, 86–107.

become a healing community that reached into our neighborhood we now had some criteria by which to assess our future activities. In the first few years after adopting our vision statement, our church council evaluated proposed actions, events or programs based on these stated commitments. One of the key goals the Council set for 1995 was to "strive to become a more receiving, welcoming, patient people, individually and as a congregation."[6]

In an age of pragmatism, wherein churches may feel pressured to measure their success according to business models that promote bigger congregations, more entertaining worship and larger buildings as the ultimate signs of success, we sought to become a community of praise, diversity, healing and service to our neighborhood, and this vision freed us to bear witness to the coming new creation, God's *adventus* in our present time.[7] Naming that direction—or that telos arising out of our theological convictions—was integral in guiding us to embrace the practices that have birthed God's renewing vision within us. But to get there, we had to break free from our complacency and our entrenched patterns of survival and seek God's transforming vision for ourselves, our church and our neighborhood.

By taking up the vision of hospitality and then adopting our language to embody that as a practice, our congregation began to recover its collective imagination for how the Spirit was leading us, within our particular context and circumstances, to express the radical welcome of Jesus to those in our midst. The practice of hospitality not only preceded the other trajectories, but also propelled us towards them. As we extended the welcome of God to each other and to our neighbors, we moved, or stumbled in some cases, towards our need to welcome one another in our diversity. Once we began to extend welcome and companionship to the poor and vulnerable, we were compelled to seek justice for our neighbors by confronting the structures that diminished and marginalized them. When we recognized our own complicity with these forces, we moved

---

6. See the 1994 *Grandview Calvary Baptist Annual Report*, 4.

7. For the importance of naming the church's telos, see Wilson, *Why Church Matters*, 11–13. For the theological idea of God's future impinging on our present reality—*adventus*—see Moltmann, *Coming of God*, 29. I find the notion of God's future impinging on our present both theologically coherent with the narrative of scripture and fruitful for affirming the worth of practices such as hospitality.

towards confession and repentance and sought God's transforming work among us. In our collective shift towards hospitality, we followed a path from self to others to God, a trajectory woven among all the practices, in which the God we turn to for help is the same God who keeps calling us forward, ever deeper into our common humanity and the divine life.

As our congregation embraced the integrating practices of welcome, diversity, justice and repentance, we began to resist the disintegrating forces of exclusion, conformity, injustice and consumerism that hold such power over our culture, and this shift has transformed our understanding of common theological ideas or terms. Instead of seeing evangelism as the act of "inviting people to become Christians," which is certainly a part of the church's mandate, we have come to understand evangelism as an announcement of what God has done through Christ to defeat the powers of darkness and death and of what God is doing now by his Spirit to bring about this new life among us until the great day of complete transformation. Salvation does not refer to personal conversion alone, but rather describes God's redeeming work in Christ to restore the whole world— indeed, the whole of creation—to Shalom. Justice, in God's economy, has less to do with giving others what is their due, than with extending God's vision of Shalom over the world, which often calls us to take less so that others may have more and to extend mercy where punishment is due. By studying and engaging with the Scriptures, our church has been led to embrace God's life-giving vision of renewal for the whole of creation through Jesus by the power of the Spirit.

Apart from our continued return to and interaction with this renewed vision of the gospel, we run the risk of slipping into an old dualism and losing the dynamic quality of integration that has characterized our church. It intrigues me that we did not look at the marks of New Monasticism or the Emergent Church and try to copy them; instead, we took our neighborhood and the gospel seriously, and these marks common to other new-monastic communities emerged among us as well.

While mentoring others in these specific practices is needed as we move into the future, we will need to continue to listen to God and God's story as well as listen to our neighbor's story if we want to live out the incarnational pattern of the gospel. Otherwise, there is the danger that these practices will either subtly slip into a legalistic attempt to set us apart from other churches or reify into "the way we do church" apart from a fresh theological imagination. Succumbing to these dangers is likely to turn these trajectories into "external goods."

To avoid these dangers, we will need to remember that these practices are not the product of our will or determination but a response to the divine initiative, a response to the one who precedes our projects and pursuits. From this perspective, theological vision is like the magnet that pulls us back on course into receiving this new life in Christ, shaping the very practices we are pursuing. We are, after all, a church with a vision to first "receive and [then] extend the radical welcome of God in Christ for the transformation of our neighborhood."[8] As Volf reminds us: "The Christian life is not first about human *doing*, but about human *receiving*."[9]

While this theological narrative has shaped our practices and must continue to do so, the practices themselves have also shaped our theological understanding. By extending the welcome of God offered to us in Christ towards others, for example, we have come to see God's welcome to us with fresh eyes. By welcoming the poor and vulnerable, we have become, first, aware that we often do not believe that God is near us when we are vulnerable, and then, secondly, we have slowly come to be reassured, in our hearts and minds, that God comes nearer to us in our own poverty and vulnerability. By confessing our idolatries and experiencing transformation over time, we have come to believe in God's transforming power among us as a dynamic reality. Beliefs apart from practices can become sterile, fragmented and lose their formational power. Theological vision—a narrative that has an end goal within the particular context we inhabit—forms good practices.[10] Good practices, in turn, reveal the gaps between our beliefs and actions, reshaping our beliefs. Amy Plantinga Pauw describes well the relationship between beliefs and practices:

> Beliefs about God are not pure truths grasped by a Cartesian ego and then "applied" to the messy, ambiguous realm of practice. Religious beliefs are interwoven with a larger set of other beliefs and embedded in particular ways of life. They are couched in the language, conceptuality and history of a particular people and re-

---

8. This is the vision statement of GCBC that appears in the weekly bulletin.

9. Volf, "Theology as a Way of Life," 254.

10. See Wilson, *Living Faithfully in a Fragmented World*, 58–60.

flect personal and communal experience and desires. Religious beliefs shape and are shaped by religious practices.[11]

In reviewing our history, it is apparent that theological vision and gospel-shaped practices together, like a husband and wife bound in a covenant relationship, bring new life.

> *It has always struck me as having something more of a casting of a vision of involvement and engagement in the neighborhood and its concerns that calls on people to respond in a variety of ways and so in that sense isn't just sort of something that is real leader-driven and individual kind of charisma driving the thing but a sort of social and theological vision that encourages and prods people to take up and be involved. So in that sense it is a kind of collective thing and lots of people individually are participating in that shared collective vision in a variety of different ways.*

Instead of relying upon conformity of belief to maintain the unity of our church, our common practices have become a building block in our foundation, freeing us to live with considerable theological diversity while still remaining united around our allegiance to Jesus. What is more, these practices themselves offer us resources to work through controversial theological issues: they summon us to welcome the one with whom we disagree, listen to the one whose story differ from our own and consider the voice of the most vulnerable when we would like to trumpet our own.

Another gift of these common practices is the concrete expression they have given to the life of discipleship, both for those who are new to the life of faith and for those seeking to recover a more meaningful Christianity. By sharing in these common practices, a greater number of people from our church have become "actors instead of bystanders": they have found their part in this mission and taken responsibility for their own responses.[12] While this shift has required a higher level of involvement and commitment than many people expected when they became a part of the church, it has empowered people to perceive the Spirit's gifting and power to help them participate in God's restoring action in the world.

---

11. Plantinga Pauw, "Attending to the Gap between Beliefs and Practices," 36.

12. Bauman, *Society Under Siege,* 201–21 discusses how the forces of our society push people in the opposite direction.

The notion that these practices can contribute to our personal formation as humans *over time* runs contrary to the cultural notion that we can quickly alter our character, and that we can do it merely through our own manipulations and will. In her writing about the wisdom of Benedictine practices, Joan Chittister comments on how hard it is for people in our culture to believe that these practices of prayer, scripture reading, stability, poverty, and obedience will shape our lives over time, over a period of longer than a weekend seminar.[13]

We have witnessed this slow transformation in the course of pursuing our shared practices. Whereas some of us began with a view of sharing our lives that looked more like quick incursions into enemy territory, we have now grown to be comfortable in being together, like wounded patients recovering together in a hospital ward. Whereas some of us previously viewed our homes as private havens to block out the world, we have now come to view them more as schools, where we learn to love and welcome strangers. Whereas fear and suspicion often dominated our interactions with people of other cultures, we have gravitated towards a hermeneutic of trust with newcomers from another culture.[14] Whereas some of us merely theorized about the need to seek justice for the least, we have now taken action.

All these transforming perspectives have occurred in increments, tiny steps over the past twenty years, with one response leading to the next along a particular trajectory. If these practices are going to take root and flourish among us, we will need to continually recognize the great distance we still need to travel. And if we are going to remain a united and hospitable community, those who have been living out these practices longer will need to extend grace and love to those who are just beginning the journey.

> You are constantly needing to provide a safe place for people for
> whom this transformation is possibly threatening and so I think that
> slows the movement down and I don't know that that is necessarily
> a bad thing, because the bottom line is that it is relational.

13. Chittister, *Wisdom Distilled from the Daily*, 6. Chittister maintains this argument throughout the book but discusses it explicitly in the introduction.

14. See Ricouer, *Conflict of Interpretation,* wherein he advocates a dialectic between a hermeneutics of trust and a hermeneutics of suspsicion as a way of moving towards understanding and truth.

By patiently mentoring those who are just beginning to live out the gospel narrative's transforming vision, we will not only sustain these trajectories within the life of our own church, but may find that we are contributing to the mission of God in ways beyond our current imagination.[15]

15. See Wilson, *Living Faithfully in a Fragmented World*, 58–60.

FIVE

Navigating the Rapids of Fear, Suspicion, and Alienation

We, who hated and killed one another and would not associate with men of different tribes because of different customs, now after the manifestation of Christ, live together and pray for our enemies and try to persuade those who unjustly harm us, so that they, living according to the fair command of Christ, may share with us the good hope of receiving the same things from God, the Master of all.[1]

While some might be threatened by the increasing diversity of our urban centers, churches are poised to view such diversity as an opportunity to practice the reconciling work of Christ and to discover the beauty of the image of God in all people. Over the past four decades, GCBC has shifted from a homogenous congregation to a diverse one towards an integrated multicultural body sharing life together in our particular urban context.[2] Our movement along this trajectory has been less linear than the previous movement towards radical hospitality. While there has been steady growth in our common understanding of what it means to pursue this

1. Justin, the Martyr, "First Apology of Justin the Martyr," 249–50.

2. The word multicultural seems to have morphed in popular usage into a catch-all term for racial, ethnic and cultural or sub-cultural diversity. I am using the term to refer primarily to ethnic and racial diversity, although as I mention below, sub-cultural forms of diversity are also present in our congregations and contribute to the challenges of being the church together. I also recognize that the word "culture" is notoriously difficult to define. I am using the word to denote the shared practices, convictions, institutions and narratives that order and give shape to the lives of a particular group of people.

practice of a shared, multicultural life, there have also been times when we have become alienated from one another, and it's felt as if we were paddling in circles without getting anywhere. But these awkward eddies seem to be characteristic of multicultural churches everywhere, and as one woman reported in a research study of our church, she *"trusted the vision and can live with the awkwardness."*[3]

The racial and ethnic homogeneity of GCBC's past is not simply something from a bygone era, for most church congregations today still reflect this homogenous composition.[4] Among many Evangelical denominations, racial and cultural segregation was even promoted as the best way to facilitate church growth via the homogeneous unit principle.[5] The quip that Sunday morning is America's most segregated hour continues to name the reality for the majority of our ecclesiastical gatherings.[6]

But the biblical narrative traces the movement from one "culturally segregated" nation towards a community composed of every "tribe, nation, language and people."[7] Jesus crosses cultural and social boundaries in his public ministry, engaging and welcoming those who were lepers, Samaritans and even Romans, Israel's enemies.[8] The gospels tell the story of Jesus as the climax of Israel's story, the story of a nation called to overcome evil and bless all the nations of the world.[9] After his resurrection, Jesus confirms that the story of God's salvation has taken this climactic

---

3. See Pearce, *Characteristics of Emerging Healthy Multicultural Churches*, 106–7. Pearce studied three multicultural churches, two in Vancouver and one in Toronto around 1996. GCBC was one of the Vancouver churches. Pearce interviewed eleven people from our church in his study, including two Latin Americans, two Asians and seven Caucasians. I will allude to some of the findings and conclusions from that study in this chapter.

4. An extensive study of American congregations in 1999 revealed that only 8 percent of all churches were multiracial at that time (which, for this study's purposes, meant black and white together. See Yancey, *One Body, One Spirit*, 15.) While the racial landscape in Canada is less focused on the Black/White majorities, I suspect from my observations that the Canadian churches are similar. I have not been able to find any substantial statistics on the racial composition of Canadian churches.

5. See McGavran, *Understanding Church Growth*.

6. Martin Luther King Jr. offered this observation in a number of his speeches.

7. Rev 7:9.

8. See Luke 17:1–19, John 4, and Matthew 8 for examples of each one of these.

9. See Wright, *New Testament and the People of God*, 371–410.

turn, sending his followers to preach this good news to all the nations of the earth, making disciples among every group.[10]

The concrete expression of this new community moved closer to reality when Peter came to realize that "God does not show favouritism but accepts people from every nation who call out to him,"[11] and then Paul envisioned the church as the new humanity[12] made of Jew and Greek, slave and free, men and women,[13] a sign bearing witness to God's reconciliation through Christ.[14] The thrust of the biblical story moves persistently towards this multicultural vision. The segregation stretching back to the earliest pages of scripture at the tower of Babel[15] is confronted by the gospel message of reconciliation. The uniting work of the Spirit at Pentecost calls the church to overcome divisions—cultural, ethnic, and racial—and embody God's reconciliation achieved through Christ.[16] As the nations of the world continue to move cross-nationally to the cities of the world, church communities will need to seek God's healing for the divisions within our countries by taking up the gospel's vision for the peace and flourishing of all things in Christ.

FROM HOMOGENEITY TO DIVERSITY

> I looked and there was a great multitude that no one could count,
> from every nation, from all tribes and peoples and languages,
> standing before the throne and before the lamb. (Rev 7:9)

Currently, the composition of our two congregations draws from thirty countries among six continents.[17] Within that ethnic mix are numerous

10. Matt 28:18–20.

11. Acts 10:34–35.

12. Col 3:10.

13. Gal 3:28.

14. Ephesians 2.

15. Genesis 11.

16. For an insightful exploration of postmodern culture's interaction with the gospel that compares and contrasts the stories of Babel and Pentecost, see Middleton and Walsh, *Truth is Stranger than it Used to Be*.

17. Our church functions with two congregations that both share the vision of the church but which develop their worshipping life somewhat differently. We have a shared council composed of leaders from both congregations. We worship and eat together five or six times a year and share in many other common ventures and events.

races, and for many, English is not their first language. The three hundred people who make up our congregations come from widely varied educational, economic and social backgrounds and include those who live on or near the street and those who teach in universities or serve in leadership roles in business and social services. There are many people struggling to make a living and a few struggling to figure out how to give away their money well.

But the church did not use to be so diverse, for when one congregant joined thirty-eight years ago, there was only one non-white member. Grandview and Calvary Baptist began to shift towards greater diversity shortly after they amalgamated in 1970 and called a pastor of Japanese-Canadian ancestry. Though they slowly began to welcome other racial and ethnic groups, some of those didn't stay long-term. One congregant who joined the church from the Calvary group gives this broad sweep of the church's intercultural history:

> It is only E. who didn't fit in [back in 1970]. When we came from Calvary, there were the N.'s—they were probably the only Asians— and then that group of Indonesians came. There was quite a group of them and all their friends. And then the Spanish came and they left, and now we don't have any dominant group, I don't think. We are all mixed in, a few of these, a few of those.

When I arrived in 1989, the church was certainly moving towards ethnic and racial diversity, though the congregation was not yet very diverse socially or theologically. There were about five or six races represented, along with people who had immigrated from other countries in the previous decade. However, there was only a minimal attempt to acknowledge, express, appreciate or critique the different ethnic backgrounds. Our worship, theology and mission seemed to be little affected by the presence of other cultures. People were seldom invited to share their own cultural histories, practices or art in our public gatherings. There was some acknowledgment of how our cultural backgrounds shape our perspective, such as in our discussions about the type of leadership needed in our church, but not much. David Anderson disputes that the presence of multiple cultures or races alone makes a church multicultural: "Multiple colours of skin within a church do not a multicultural church make! A vibrant multicultural church allows multiple cultures freedom of expression through a variety of art forms."[18]

But the presence of people from other countries brought together those who were visible minorities and immigrants within the congregation, as they shared camaraderie in their experience of being misunderstood and also in their struggle to adapt to a new culture. One woman, the lone congregant with her particular national and ethnic origin, told me that this shared experience with other immigrants gave her a greater sense of fitting in, despite the solitary status of her own ethnic group. This viewpoint was reiterated by a number of immigrants or people of visible minorities when we hired a Black African pastor from Burundi.[19] Similarly, a man from Bangladesh remarked how valuable our youth pastor's experience as the daughter of a man who immigrated from Tunisia has been to him: *"Yes, N. is really in a good position. She understands what is happening. She understands us as parents."*

During our visioning process in 1993 and 1994, we were led to name the multicultural vision as part of our church's mission, and we committed ourselves to be "a church which reflects the richness and diversity of our urban neighborhood and God's kingdom" and "a community of healing and discipleship." We began to celebrate our cultural diversity in our anniversary celebrations, and multiculturalism became a theme of our summer day camps.[20] With Vancouver's diverse cultural mix and the church's growing diversity, we embraced what we believed was the call of God for our church: to move towards greater diversity in our shared life. But we didn't get there without learning some hard lessons first.

Making Mistakes

In the fall of 1991, a few years into my pastoral tenure, our church received a request from a local refugee agency (with which I had developed a good relationship) to supply Christmas gift hampers for twenty-six Latin American families, mostly from Guatemala, El Salvador, Honduras, and

18. Anderson, *Multicultural Ministry*, 110.

19. Many of these folks are in intercultural marriages, a subject which I will discuss later.

20. The annual reports for the years 1993–1996 name this theme repeatedly.

Nicaragua. Refugees fleeing the civil wars in those regions had been set-tling in the Grandview Woodlands neighborhood throughout the previ-ous decade since there were social services and cheaper rentals. A number of those families showed up at our worship services around Christmas, exposing us to the presence of this population group and piquing our imagination as to whether we could be together as one church, espe-cially since a number of these guests expressed interest in being involved. Spanish speakers were not represented in our church before this time, and our congregation's welcome of these strangers opened us to seeing them as "the neighbour I have not loved, the alien in my midst" rather than "people who were *not like us.*"[21]

A few months later, we were able to hire A., a seminary student who had recently arrived from Venezuela with her husband. (Eventually, we hired them both, since A.'s husband couldn't find other work.) A. and O. moved into the basement of our house next to the church and started making connections with those Spanish-speaking families. Since many of these families had sparse English skills (including O. himself), A. began translating the sermons in the pews, and then later decided to leave the sanctuary after the first half of our worship in order to teach/preach in Spanish with this small group downstairs. Difficulties in speaking and learning English would remain a primary issue in our relationship with and ministry among these Spanish speakers, many of whom did not em-brace our intercultural model.

Dealing with language differences is a perplexing issue for churches seeking to welcome new immigrants from non-English speaking coun-tries. On the one hand, immigrants to North America will need to devel-op English skills, so participating in worship and in an English-speaking church is one way to facilitate that language acquisition and societal inte-gration. To assist with that process, we began to teach English classes, par-ticularly to children, whose parents were keen for them to learn English.[22] While many immigrants appreciated our help as well as our desire to include them in worship, they still gravitated towards Spanish-speaking preaching and resisted English-speaking environments. This was due, in

21. Rice, "Lamenting Racial Divisions," 61.

22. A man from Bangladesh expresses what many immigrants and refugees have told me. "*Those who come to Canada come for the next generation because we do not see any hope for the next generation in our country. So the kids are the main concern.*"

part, to the fatigue involved in trying to understand a second language, but some felt that their intelligence was undermined by not being able to communicate in English (or thought that others deemed them less intelligent, which did happen on occasion). Others felt that they could not pray or sing in a meaningful way in English, since it was not their first language. Still others were concerned that their children would lose their original language and culture if they did not speak Spanish at church. As a result of these difficulties, some of the Latin Americans expressed a desire to build up a sizeable enough Spanish-speaking group so that they could start their own church.

About six months after A. and O. moved back to Venezuela, we hired R., who was from Mexico. His personable style of ministry and gifts of leadership led to a growing Hispanic cohort within our church. Though we worshipped together for the entire Sunday morning and had a Spanish-speaking Bible study following lunch, there were growing tensions, since R. remained unconvinced about our multicultural model. While he appreciated the opportunity to develop his pastoral skills in this setting, he struggled to embrace the model himself. After a couple of years, he began to discuss with individuals within the Spanish-speaking group, as well as with another Spanish church, the possibility of planting a Spanish-speaking church in the area. After serving with us for more than three years, he came to me one morning and said that if we did not support him in planting this church, he would plant it with the other church, where he had begun worshipping the previous year.

This announcement left many of us discouraged, particularly when half of the twenty people in that group joined R. Not surprisingly, most of those who joined R. were Mexican, and most who stayed were Central American, which confirmed the division that had been growing within the group along cultural lines. (At the outset of R.'s hiring, I had naively underestimated the cultural distinctiveness and division between most Mexicans and Central Americans).

In retrospect, I learned how important it is to draw our leaders from other cultures into the center of our church's leadership so that they will be exposed to the challenges that the entire church experiences in pursuing this intercultural model. A. and O. may have had a different perspective on their own ministry with Latin Americans if they could have observed, from the inside, the genuine attempts that leadership was making to guide the whole church toward this mutual embrace. Moreover, I became the conduit between the deacons and A. and O., which caused miscommunication and personal animosity towards me whenever I had "bad news" to communicate from the council. In an attempt to rectify this triangulation, R. was immediately invited onto Council when he became a pastor.

Theological differences over our church's movement towards intercultural community were also a hurdle, and we learned from this experience the importance of discussing our theological differences before hiring any staff.[23] Both R. and O. (and to a lesser extent A.) disagreed in significant measure with our wider, kingdom theology and did not value theological training. In his extensive study of interracial churches, George Yancey concludes that "theological differences on a congregational staff are much more deadly to the cohesiveness of that staff than racial differences."[24] He also suggests that it would be better to be patient in hiring someone with a better theological fit rather than hiring someone with significant theological differences.

Yet the outcome of this painful fissure with R. was that we shifted from a predominately bi-cultural model to a multicultural vision. As one of our members expressed, *"The Spanish left, and now we don't have any dominant group, I don't think. We are all mixed in, a few of these, a few of those."*

A Second Chance

Two-thirds of the way through this bi-cultural stage (when almost one-quarter of the congregation was Hispanic), seven newly-arrived Burmese refugee claimants showed up for worship one Sunday through a connection with a refugee agency whose director I had gotten to know.[25] These

23. While we didn't discuss our theological vision for multicultural ministry in detail with A. and O., partially because we had not articulated our vision nor embraced racial diversity as a commitment yet, we did discuss these issues with R. before we hired him. What we failed to discuss, however, was what we thought this pathway would require of each of us.

24. Yancey, *One Body, One Spirit,* 96.

25. These statistics and the challenge of becoming more multicultural were named in my pastoral report that year for the church (1995).

newcomers from the Karen ethnic group were familiar with Baptists, since they are the predominate Christian group working among their people.

Rather than trying to find someone Burmese to pastor them (as we had with the Latin American refugees), I took the pastoral lead. As I visited with them in the next few weeks, I discovered that they wanted to start a Bible study in which they would translate from English into Karen (and later into Burmese, when we added Burmese who were not of Karen ethnic heritage). I decided to lead this group myself, first going on my own, then inviting a student to come with me, who in turn assumed leadership of the group and invited others to join him. J., one of the Burmese newcomers, mentioned the pastors and P., the student leader, as the most important people in making her feel welcome. Having an already integrated member link that first new person from a racial, ethnic or cultural minority into the church community was and is critical to the integration of newly arrived immigrants.[26]

These bi-weekly Saturday night gatherings changed me as I heard the stories of their struggle to survive during their flight from Burma and their dangerous, protracted stay in the refugee camps of Thailand. As I listened to them talk about their devotion and compassion for one other through these hardships, I grew to admire and love these new friends. Even though I often felt like staying home most of these Saturday nights, as I had other evening responsibilities throughout the week, I came away from those gatherings grateful, refreshed and rooted, as I had been relieved of some of the superficial preoccupations of middle-class North Americans for a few hours. I also became more aware of the innumerable hurdles that immigrants (particularly refugees) face as they try to establish a new life in a new country and culture, without much English.

Eventually, several members of this group moved farther away and they began to connect with a little Burmese group that was forming closer to their homes. A few of the remaining members formed a new home group with the student leader and others from our church, including our new pastor, an experience that helped draw the refugees into the center of the church as they participated more fully in the life of the community. J. described her relationship with the new pastor as *warm and safe*" and

26. David Anderson concurs with this conclusion. See Anderson, *Multicultural Ministry*, 110–13.

said, "*I like my church. Both pastors and the congregation are close spiritually with me. I like the people. They cared a lot for me.*"

Since this couple had fled Burma without their four-year old son, the congregation began to pray for their reunification and grew to cherish this family. When their son finally arrived five years later, the entire congregation joined in this joyful celebration, leaving the nine-year-old boy a little stunned by all the attention. J. describes how she felt about that period of waiting and eventual celebration: "*It was important. Something touched me. People cared so deeply for me. I felt like they had become brothers and sisters in Christ.*" This family contributed their music, leadership abilities (the husband became a deacon), and began to connect us to other Burmese families. When one of their Burmese acquaintances was in hospital suffering from complications due to HIV that he contracted in the refugee camps in Thailand, my pastoral colleague and her husband went to pray with him, after which he became a Christian and also became part of the church.

In retrospect, we can see how our decision to hire someone to lead and care for the Latin Americans among us distanced them from the rest of the congregation and prevented the leadership from building relationships with them, which led to a segregated congregation. With the Burmese immigrants, I facilitated relationships between them and other congregants, which increased the connections we had with one another, so that their group did not relate to the rest of the congregation through only one leader.

It is also important to recognize that some new immigrants will not want to or perhaps even be able to integrate into a multicultural setting. Those who are just starting to learn English are often so disoriented that they long for the comfort of familiarity with their own cultural group, and even those who have integrated still enjoy being with others who share a common history, culture or first language (as most of us do). A couple from Bangladesh who have been part of the church for ten years and who have integrated well recently began a culturally distinct fellowship for other Bengalis, but when connected with a multicultural church and leaders who are themselves integrating, such culturally distinct fellowships can be a stepping stone towards greater integration.[27]

27. See Pearce, "Characteristics," 138–39.

FROM DIVERSITY TOWARDS INTEGRATED MULTICULTURAL LIVING

> When mutual tolerance is coupled with indifference, communal cultures may live alongside each other, but seldom talk to each other. . . . In a world of multiculturalism, cultures may coexist but it is hard for them to benefit from a shared life.[28]

We have been able to move from diversity towards a shared, integrated life in part because we are a small church with a commitment to community, which continually places us in proximity to each other, whether in our worship gatherings, around a meal afterwards, at a church meeting, on a church retreat, or in one of our home groups. In our society, or even a large church, people from differing cultural groups can work together, live next to one another or sit beside one another in a church pew and remain relatively distant from one another. Our intentional commitment to a shared life as a small community exposes many of our false stereotypes of others and launches us on a trajectory of human encounter and discovery. Since our growth has been slow, from about sixty to a hundred and twenty congregants in my first decade, there has been plenty of time for these personal, face-to-face encounters.[29]

During an annual church retreat, a man from Honduras told me that it was the first time he had spent more than a few minutes speaking with people who were not Latin American. At another retreat, a family from Columbia became Christ-followers shortly after their experience of welcome and inclusion from so many different people. During our 1996 retreat, after a group of people who reflected the growing ethnic and racial diversity in our church each declared that there was *"no one like me,"* they were surprised to hear that the Caucasian folks felt the same way, since they perceived that there was no one else in their specific age range, or no one who shared their life interests. This observation, which was expressed as a deficit, turned into a hopeful discovery when we realized that we were becoming a community of people despite our differences. When another

---

28. Bauman, *Community*, 135

29. Higher expectations of friendship in churches versus workplaces or schools can also make these friendships tricky to sustain, as George Yancey argues in *One Body, One Spirit*, 28.

person is encountered in shared humanity, as one jointly fashioned in the image of God and as a fellow member of Christ's body, there is ground upon which to build friendship, however different we may perceive others to be from ourselves.[30]

Within home groups, as people met in each other's homes over meals, Scripture, and prayer, trust and friendship began to replace suspicion and strangeness. By the mid-90s, we had seven home groups, and five were multi-ethnic and multiracial. The global composition of one group included people from Burma, Cameroon, El Salvador, Australia, Denmark, and Bangladesh, as well as a few home-brewed Canadians, causing the group to joke that they just need to find a penguin and then they could boast of having someone from every continent.

Our family experienced the gifts of cross-cultural friendships as well. When a Bangladeshi man phoned the church one Saturday night, where I was working in my office scrambling to finish my sermon for Sunday, he inquired about the start time for the service, and I arranged a pick-up for his family. Their two children, similar in ages to our two oldest, soon became friends, and over the last decade, we have become like family, referring to each other with the monikers "uncle, aunt, cousins" and sharing in birthdays and holiday celebrations. When we were first welcomed into their home, our delight and preference for their ethnic cuisine both surprised and delighted them. When they welcomed us into their Bangladeshi community's celebration of their Independence Day, our then nine-year-old son joined their son and about fifteen other children on the stage to wave flags during the performance of a nationally known song. Our son didn't even notice that he was the lone Caucasian kid participating in this rite in front of about two hundred Bangladeshis: what he knew was that he was up there with his friend S.

Out of these cross-cultural friendships, those who have been welcomed feel cared for and find a secure sense of belonging and can then, in turn, extend that welcome and concern to others, particularly those from other cultures. One immigrant confirms this shift in his own life.

30. See Volf, *Exclusion and Embrace*, 125–67. Volf explores in depth both of these reasons to move toward the other. See also Milne, *Dynamic Diversity*, 55–73 for other reasons why we can and should develop a common life among differing cultures such as the communal life of the Trinity, the reconciliation achieved on the cross and the future community awaiting us at the eschaton for which we are to prepare now.

> *After ten years now, I appreciate that I am in a multi-cultural situation . . . It broadens my idea and opens my eyes to see and to understand and to accept. Also before I was just considering what I am getting from the church but now I think about what everybody is getting from the church because if it is a multi-cultural church, everybody needs to be noticed, everybody needs to enter in, everybody needs to be ministered to. It is not only me, which it was in the beginning.*

Throughout the 90s, our church community slowly incorporated more people from a variety of ethnic and cultural backgrounds, shaping us into an intercultural congregation. During this time, a doctoral candidate doing research on our church identified and affirmed five strengths in our move towards this shared multicultural life:

1. A shared vision based on a clear biblical understanding of God's expectation that faith communities should represent the diversity of cultures.
2. An intentional commitment to ministries with those living in the neighborhood.
3. An openness to deal with the awkwardness resulting from cultural expectations and language in church experience.
4. A concern for developing natural links to ethnic communities, here and beyond.
5. A greater concern for being an effective community than being an efficient community.[31]

These characteristics of an emerging multicultural church took root and solidified in the decade that followed as we worshipped together and continued to welcome those who were strangers into our midst.

Worshiping Together in a Multicultural Church

What does worship look like in a multicultural church? To begin with, it can be a little chaotic. Early attempts to be more inclusive included an invitation for people to pray in their first language during our public prayer times, or for people to translate for their friends in the pew

---

31. Pearce, "Characteristics," 176.

beside them, as well as opportunities for individuals to read Scripture in other languages. Over the years, particularly under the influence and leadership of my pastoral colleague and our worship coordinator, we have added culturally diverse fabric and art in our sanctuary, foreign musical instruments and international dance. We have learned a variety of songs from one another's countries, often in languages other than English. New songs written by composers in our congregations often include verses in Spanish and French as well as English. Our anniversary celebrations have become an annual opportunity to revel in the goodness of our diverse cultural backgrounds. Our worship coordinator alludes to the importance of these celebrations and to singing songs from other languages in her annual report from 2004:

> We continue to recognize that we are a diverse congregation and we try to reflect that diversity in our corporate worship. The anniversary celebration with a drum and song from members of the First nations community, dancing from Burma, songs from Japan and Burundi and costumes from many different nations was a clear example of Christ's presence in all the nations. Even though our pronunciation of the many different languages that we sing often leaves something to be desired, it continues to be important for us to sing songs from other cultures because it reminds us of the incarnation as a cross-cultural manifestation of God's presence among us—all of us.[32]

During our Easter worship, in what has become a cherished multicultural tradition, we invite people from every country represented in our congregation to stand and declare, "Christ is Risen" in their country, making this pronouncement in their first language. After each declaration, the congregation sings the refrain, "he is risen from the dead." While this act of worship may sometimes appear more symbolic than substantial, it nonetheless indicates a stance of receiving from newcomers, a stance that has an affect upon immigrants, as this man testifies:

> Of course it is not easy to know how things move from one step to another, but I would say that what you experience in the first place is that you are accepted. As years went by, I felt that of course my contribution was welcomed through songs, worship. I heard that

32. From the worship coordinator's report, *2004 GCBC Annual Report*, 16.

what we needed was your thoughts and maybe we need your minis-
try too. That is where I think that it moved towards this integrated
multi-cultural living where actually you are part of the community
and who you are becomes part of the reality of the community.

Another congregant names the attempt the church has made to welcome the contributions of our differing cultural backgrounds: "*We have tried to eliminate distinctions between class and people from different cultures, not by ignoring them but by celebrating them.*" At this point in history, with lingering suspicion and fear between so many cultures,[33] empowering others to express and perhaps even preserve their culture is important to overcoming suspicion and affirming God's image within all peoples. David Anderson articulates why we must be diligent and intentional about affirming cultures:

> Perhaps one day we can have a colorblind society. But in today's world so-called colorblindness is a denial of the fact that racial identity continues to play an important role in our lives. For many racial minorities the notion of colorblindness becomes a barrier to racial justice since it denies the reality of racism and prejudice that they face. My prayer is that the church, whether Anglo, African or Afghan, would refuse to be colour-blind. Why would we ever want to dull a sense that we've been given by our creator? Who among us would ever desire to walk through a garden to behold one colour and one kind of flower?[34]

Yet, do we sometimes see only the color of the flower and miss its other features? Perhaps there is a dialectically traveled path between highlighting the colors and focusing beyond them that will lead us towards greater intercultural understanding and cooperation. Speaking about a woman from Africa who was on our Council, another woman currently in leadership comments about the danger of limiting people's contribution by focusing on their cultural contribution:

> *We want diversity so we welcome people in but it can also so easily become tokenism. I had a conversation with S. before she left and she said she felt like people wanted to hear the African perspective where she just wanted to be seen as part of the community giving*

33. See Bauman, *Community*, 4.

34. Anderson, *Multicultural Ministry*, 119.

her perspective, which is mixed with her African experience and her experience here. I felt that way in Japan often. Somehow you have to be intentional to welcome others but the next step beyond that is then to [move to] a point that you don't see the difference.

Welcoming Immigrants

As we moved from a bi-cultural congregation to a more multicultural congregation, an influx of new immigrants came via Kinbrace, our transitional community house for refugee claimants, one of the most vulnerable of all immigrant groups. A decade ago, my pastoral colleague T., along with her husband L., moved into this seven-suite house situated seven blocks north of the church. Their hospitable and gentle approach to welcoming refugee claimants led numerous residents to become part of our church community. Their arrival not only broadened the cultural diversity of our church, but also exposed us to the structural injustice which refugees face at home and abroad.[35] Praying for people awaiting the determination of their refugee claims has aroused empathy from others in our congregation. The Tuesday night meal at Kinbrace, along with the annual Thanksgiving celebration, has effectively united Canadian and American residents with this vulnerable group and led to a community within our community, another context for face-to-face encounter and integration.[36]

Welcoming the Poor and the Vulnerable

> In developing such a missional theology it is imperative, if evangelicals wish to be closer to the biblical story instead of to contemporary consumer and middle class values, to make God's love for the poor a more central missional motif. In other words, service to the poor is not the leftovers of our generosity. It is at the heart of God and the church's mission.[37]

35. I address this subject in the next chapter.

36. To learn more about Kinbrace, you can retrieve information at http://salsbury communitysociety.com. Two years ago, Hawthorne foundation was able to purchase the house directly adjacent to Kinbrace, which has become Kinbrace 2.

37. Ringma, "Liberation Theologians," 55.

The practice of welcoming the poor and vulnerable into our midst has been central to our transformation, as it frees us from the grip of consumerism and individualism and propels us into solidarity with the least, thereby opening our eyes to the injustices within society and stirring our hearts towards action and structural change as we contend with the powers that benefit from the status quo.

While charity and justice for the poor may be regarded as admirable acts of service in our culture, the gospel invites us to discover them as pathways into knowing God's love and discovering our true humanity. Charity on its own, apart from a willingness to throw our lot in with the poor and stake our destiny with theirs, can perpetuate our sense of apathy and maintain the status quo acceptance of poverty as "just the way things are."[38]

Rather than insulating us from the pain of the world, our commitment to seek a re-ordering of our world according to the biblical vision of Shalom has kept us near our neighbors in need when we may have easily retreated into a comfortable spirituality. But the gospel invites us to take up our cross and follow Christ and to be shaped into a community that shares in the mission of God. As N. T. Wright reminds us:

> The call of the gospel is for the church to implement the victory of God through suffering love. The cross is not just an example to be followed; it is an achievement to be worked out, put into practice. But it is an example nonetheless, because it is the exemplar—the template, the model—for what God now wants to do by his Spirit in the world through his people. It is the start of the process of redemption, in which suffering and martyrdom are the paradoxical means by which victory is won.[39]

This awareness of individual and communal suffering has caused fatigue and, at times, despair among the people of our congregation, particularly when we see housing prices in our neighborhood driving the poor among us onto the streets. And yet, as Christine Pohl observes, "faithful hospitality usually involves laying our lives down in little pieces, in small acts of sacrificial love and service. Part of the mystery is that while

---

38. This is a shared critique of much liberation theology. See Gutierrez, *Liberation Theology*, especially 163.

39. Wright, *Evil and the Justice of God*, 98.

such concrete acts of love are costly, they nourish and heal both giver and recipient."[40] These everyday experiences of shared suffering have become a doorway to God's healing and restoration as we discover our common humanity with the least among us.

Diverse Leadership

As our congregations have moved further along the path towards sharing an integrated and multicultural life, we have discovered the importance of having a diverse leadership who are committed to developing meaningful relationships with newcomers from other countries, deliberately welcoming them to participate and contribute to our life together.

In a study of multicultural churches, Yancey identifies the successful churches as those that have leaders who are skilled in cross-cultural relations and are intentional about this role.[41] But even more critical was his discovery that multiracial churches had, in the vast majority of cases, developed multiracial leadership, at least among lay people if not among the staff.[42] From his own research, David Anderson draws the same conclusion: "Multicultural churches had multicultural staffs, while uni-cultural churches did not. In other words, those who led multicultural churches staffed their leadership team to reflect the diversity they already had or desired to have in their congregation."[43]

When our congregation called T. as the co-pastor of our church, we modeled this diversity and reconciling vision of the gospel, since her presence and pastoral leadership was a source of healing for many women. *"It was . . . very healing for me to have a place where we had a woman pastor and that has been healing from my past church experiences."*

For the past two decades, diverse and multiracial leadership has been a relative constant of GCBC's story, both among lay leaders (worship leaders, committee heads, program/ ministry leaders and council, where we have deliberately sought to reflect the ethnic composition of our community) and our paid and pastoral staff: from our Japanese-Canadian pastor

40. Pohl, *Making Room*, 34.

41. Yancey discusses these two traits in *One Body, One Spirit*, 108–27.

42. Yancey, *One Body, One Spirit*, 87.

43. Anderson, *Multicultural Ministry*, 166.

during the 1970s and 80s to a Venezuelan pastor during the early 90s to a
Mexican pastor during the mid-90s, to our present staff, which includes
our Canadian-Chinese children's ministry coordinator and our Burundi
co-pastor (who came to Canada as a refugee and has had residency for
only five years).

This decision to hire a recent immigrant to a position of overall pastoral leadership was identified by many people as a step of progress in
implementing our multicultural vision as a church.

> I am quite fascinated to watch E. He just approaches things differ-
> ently. He preaches differently in some subtle ways and some more
> overt ways . . . To have someone who is actually a pastor from a
> different culture—it will be interesting to see how that bears out.

> It is one thing to have people from other cultures within our church
> community but to invite somebody into a position of leadership [is
> significant] because they will start to change things.

Another person affirms the congregation's decision to choose a recent immigrant as a pastor, but is not convinced that we are ready to have
our culture as a church transformed: "*I wonder how much we really want
them to shake things up or change things.*" The future will tell us whether we
were ready or not, as we move further along the trajectory of embracing a
more integrated multicultural life together.

Theological Diversity

As ideologies fragment and individualistic approaches to faith flourish,
it will be difficult for churches to expect theological agreement among
their members.[44] At GCBC, the pastoral leadership has tried to articulate a theological vision of the kingdom that incorporates these differing theological perspectives into a more unified whole, making space for
dialogue regarding our differences, trusting that the Holy Spirit will guide
us into truth as a community.[45] As one member explains, "*We are working
towards something different. I am not going to be threatened if this other*

44. See Bibby, *Mosaic Madness.*

45. In a personal conversation, Bakke said that it is important for pastors to have a
large kingdom vision, larger than most of their members, if they are going to be able to
draw people into a unified mission.

person has a very different perspective. And part of [the reason for] that is a theology of diversity."

When the U.S. began the war with Iraq in 2004, one of our members put up a sign in the church parking lot that said, "No To War" (in response to a bulletin insert inviting people to respond in some way to the war). When someone asked Council to take down the sign since the church hadn't discussed this response together, Council decided to ask the member to remove the sign, which he did. We then organized a night where we listened to a presentation on the history of Christian responses to war and invited people to share their experiences around war in small group discussions, which broke through the polarized positions that people held as we began to hear and empathize with these stories. I remember hearing one woman, who was opposed to war, describe how grateful and relieved she was when Canadian soldiers came to protect their village during WWII. While disagreement lingered on after this night, the issue became less divisive in our community. Like any family, the opportunity to articulate our perspective and to hear the perspective of others stimulated understanding and trust.

Our resolve to practice this way of being the church is being tested now around issues of sexuality, especially homosexuality. While some are resolute about making more room for those involved in homosexual relationships, others feel strongly that the practice of chastity and/or heterosexual marriage should be a pre-requisite to church membership, or at least leadership. While many churches and denominations have split over disagreements about how to respond to those practicing a homosexual lifestyle, we are determined not to follow that route.[46] To prevent disintegration, we offered two preaching series around sexuality and same-gender attraction, two seminars and extended opportunities for discussion. Still, we will need to host more opportunities for members to dialogue openly about sexuality, since this experience is at the core of our humanity.

If we heed the words of two people in our church, one focusing on listening to one another's stories, the other focusing on listening to the

---

46. Part of the difficulty is that these differences extend into families themselves wherein the younger generation tends to be more affirming of homosexual practice. This difference is even wider in most immigrant families I have spoken with.

story of Scripture, perhaps there is hope that we can find our way to a place of mutual transformation.

> *When I keep hearing people's experiences, that is, when I have to come back to my theology and have to wrestle with "wow, what do I do with their experience and my theology?"*

> *I think that with our background from an evangelical tradition, that [biblical theology] is a touchstone point of security for everybody, or almost everybody; the biblical and theological framework is so key to giving people a sense of "it's okay." This has been important at Grandview and I trust it will continue to be. It is not about following some element of the latest trend, social or political, which I think kind of the more progressive attempts at being inclusive have often been aligned, wherein people find themselves panicking that they are falling outside the realm of orthodox evangelical faith. The more we can use the language in an authentic and integrated way, and the tradition—you know hymns, the devotion, everything that gives people a sense of who we are and what we are on about—but expanding the vision of that in a biblical and theological way and moving from within that larger milieu towards some of these things that translate into social and political decisions on the ground, then people will have ground to stand on.*[47]

Holding these two together—genuine openness to the other and genuine openness to Scripture—will certainly stretch us, but if we are to navigate through this complex issue and remain a united, missional community, then we will need to demonstrate a commitment to solidarity over and above conformity.[48]

47. Four seminary students, one of whom was part of our congregation, did a study of how our "missional" church could respond well to this growing area of tension in our congregations around the issue of homosexuality. They came to similar conclusions: they indicated that the leadership would do well to prepare the congregation for this dialogue by teaching on the holistic reading of Scripture (as opposed to proof-texting or ignoring the text altogether) and on the church as a family who struggles together through perplexing decisions but remains a family.

48. In "Characteristics," 164, Pearce names solidarity as a higher value than conformity.

The Gospel's Critique and Affirmation of All Cultures

As we seek to embrace a more integrated multicultural life together, we will need to resist attempting to *assimilate* people from other cultures (or those who share differing theological beliefs) into our congregation, and instead open ourselves to being transformed together into a new perspective, a new narrative and a new praxis, one that owes its allegiance to the new world God is creating in Christ, rather than the narratives and practices of our particular culture (or sub-culture).[49] "The distance born out of our allegiance to God's future does two important services. First, it creates space in us to receive the other. . . . The second function of the distance forged by the Spirit of new creation is no less important: it entails a judgment against evil in every culture."[50] As those who share an allegiance to the gospel, which both critiques and affirms aspects of every culture,[51] the members of our church have had the opportunity to rub shoulders with people from a variety of cultures, thereby discovering goodness in others' (and in our own) cultures, as well as the hidden dehumanizing forces in our cultural frameworks.

In a recent East Side Story Guild presentation,[52] the story of Philip, the jailor in Acts 16, was woven together with the story of an imprisoned church leader in China. This juxtaposition opened new vistas into the tragic suffering and courageous faith in both stories, helping those of us outside China to better understand the type of faith and sacrificial devotion that has shaped Chinese Christianity in this century. In another presentation, the Jewish exile was interspersed with the story of the conquest and oppression of the First Nations people in our own nation and province. While acknowledging that these two stories are not parallels,[53]

49. Volf, *Exclusion and Embrace*, 50–51.

50. Ibid., 51–52.

51. Newbigin, *Gospel in a Pluralist Society*, 127.

52. The East Side Story Guild (ESSG) is an inter-generational guild that creatively uses art, music and drama to teach and then present stories of the Bible. These presentations over the last decade have shaped our imaginations with their creative telling of the Biblical narrative.

53. See the program for "Singing an Old Song in New Land," 11. The program guide notes two differences: First Nations groups were exiles in their own land (as opposed to the Jews who were removed from their land) and the First Nations do not view their exile as due to their own sinfulness (as did the Jewish exilic literature, at least on one level).

the ESSG directors did find convincing reasons for interweaving these two cultural narratives together in the place where "our story and God's story meet":[54]

> Despite these obvious differences, it was the similarities in experiences of exile that most impressed themselves upon us. A number of the First Nation's elders we talked with spoke of how, even as children in residential school, they identified their own experience of lament and longing for their own homes and their own languages with that of the Hebrew people whose stories they were exposed to in these Christian schools.

The telling of this story by the children and First Nations folk from our congregation exposed us to our own province's complicity in this continuing oppression and offered us an opportunity for reconciliation from First Nation members themselves. The presentation was mutually transforming both for the First Nations presenters and for the rest of us, offering us post-exilic hope in the good news of Christ's reconciling act of love. These small steps of reconciliation underline the distance we must yet travel towards mutual understanding. One of the leaders of the ESSG shares her own discovery of the gap in our cultural understanding through working on this project:

> *I have been working with the First Nations all Fall and they just fundamentally come at everything differently. Their music is so different than ours, and yet, it is hard for us not to think that ours is somehow superior. And I don't mean that in an obvious way; I mean it in a kind of a subconscious way. So, how do you live inside your culture, your cultural norms and then how do you understand it as an idolatry to an extent that you can relinquish and be transformed?*

The gospel narrative is a universal story that weaves together all cultures in God's re-creative action in Christ, offering us an overarching or transcendent purpose and path for the work of intercultural integration. Canadian sociologist Reginald Bibby argues that Canada's official policy of multiculturalism lacks this overarching purpose, undermining Canadian unity:

54. This is the short statement of purpose for the ESSG. The following quote also comes from 11 of the program guide.

If there is no subsequent vision, no national goals, no explicit sense of coexisting for some purpose, pluralism becomes an un-inspiring end in itself. Rather than coexistence being the foundation that enables a diverse nation to collectively pursue the best kind of existence possible, coexistence degenerates into a national preoccupation. Pluralism ceases to have a cause. The result: mosaic madness.[55]

Yancey found that this transcendent purpose is also essential for churches[56] if they are going to overcome what Spencer Perkins and Chris Rice identify as "race fatigue," a disinterest arising from the fatigue of continually being deluged with issues around race or racism.[57]

In order to overcome such "mosaic madness" or "race fatigue," our multicultural vision must be rooted in the hope that it will improve the quality of our *shared* life. As we invite people from other cultures to participate in the work of being a church, we must at the same time seek a way of life together which ensures that their views or practices will be equally valued in the end, a process of intercultural transformation that requires large doses of humility.

> I still have this egoism that says that my way is the best way and my idea is still the best idea. I still have that ego but you know sometimes I do accept that there is a better way, that they are doing it better than me, handling it better than me. I do see that but still most of the time I think I am the better one.

In a cross-cultural marriage, couples are compelled to take up this process of cultural critique and affirmation continuously.[58] This is one of the reasons for the growing number of cross-cultural couples and families who have joined our church over the years: we are attempting to do together as a church what they are also doing everyday.

55. Bibby, *Mosaic Madness*, 10.

56. Yancey, *One Body, One Spirit*, 98–107.

57. Perkins and Rice, *More Than Equals*, 100.

58. Joel Crohn points out that when interracial/intercultural couples must work these issues out is when children arrive. See Crohn, *Mixed Marriages*.

The Future of Multicultural Churches

Perhaps the key element in moving a church along the trajectory from non-discriminatory inclusion towards an inclusive, multicultural body is its commitment to stay in the struggle, even through the inevitable differences and conflicts that arise within a diverse community.

> I think that at least sometimes there is a real willingness to struggle and that means no easy answers and not even an answer from top-down but it is just that we continue to live with the struggle.

For the people of GCBC, we will need to remain intentional about welcoming newcomers from other cultures and diligent about nurturing differing cultural perspectives if we are to overcome the forces of fear and suspicion that characterize human history between cultures. As another pastor explains, "I think you can't take racial diversity for granted, that you have to find ways to promote and maintain that if you want it. Otherwise, because people are minorities, by nature, they begin to feel left out."[59]

We must also recognize that our movement along this trajectory is part of a larger global trend, the shifting geographical and cultural epicenter of Christianity North to South and West to East. Philip Jenkins documents this shift in his book *The Next Christendom: The Coming of Global Christianity*: "Over the past century, the centre of gravity in the Christian world has shifted inexorably southward, to Africa, Asia and Latin America."[60] Through global migration, we are receiving immigrants into our midst who have been formed and discipled by this increasingly bold and hopeful Christianity.[61] Will we allow them to critique Western culture and illuminate the biblical text in ways that challenge our prevailing assumptions, our "social imaginaries" which lie at the core of what defines a culture?[62] Or will we assume that those who arrive already as Christians will be primarily learning from us? One recent newcomer's words serve as a relevant reminder of the challenge and hope these new perspectives can bring to our community:

59. Yancey, *One Body, One Spirit*, 110.

60. Jenkins, *Next Christendom*, 2.

61. Ibid., 77–78.

62. On social imaginaries and the way in which every culture operates with (uncontested) assumptions, see Taylor, *A Secular Age*, 171–75.

I really don't need anything. I have food, clothes. I have everything. Why do I have to expect a gift from my friends? No one thinks that that can really hinder living the kingdom of God in a deeper way, but of course it does, because that can bring clouds in my relationship with my brothers and sisters that we really don't need.

By seeking to love each other across cultures, we bear witness to the reconciling love and action of God in Christ, and we become a living parable of the passion of God for diversity in unity.[63]

We will also need to be patient as we navigate the long, winding and often choppy river towards the fulfillment of the kingdom of God, an intercultural future when all the nations will bring their treasures into the new creation united under God.[64]

There is obviously lag time on the ground because those are just huge shifts that it is almost presumptive to think that they can happen, even within our lifetime. I think it is okay for the concept to lead us, and for the ideal from scripture to lead us forward as we take our little steps that we can. Hopefully my children will take the next big ones.

63. In a personal conversation, N. T. Wright suggested to me that perhaps our church, by moving in this multicultural direction, could and should become a living parable, a mini-story revealing the larger story of God's coming kingdom.

64. Rev 21:24.

SIX

Navigating the Rapids of Blame and Indifference

*The man who wishes to exempt himself from providing for his neighbours should
deface himself and declare that he no longer wishes to be a man, for as long as we
are human creatures we must contemplate as in a mirror our face in those who are
poor, despised, exhausted, who groan under their burdens.*[1]

FROM INDIFFERENCE TOWARDS EMBRACE

Nearly two hundred years ago, John Wesley wrote: "I see us quickly developing into, not a society of bad people, but a society with people out
of touch with the suffering of the vast majority of the world's population
today—including the poor within our own country. The distance that
wealthy people are now able to put between them and the poor makes
them less likely to appreciate the need for hospitality."[2] As Shane Claiborne
writes today: "The more I've gotten to know rich folks, the more I am convinced that the great tragedy in the church is not that rich Christians do
not care about the poor, but that rich Christians do not know the poor."[3]
Similarly, a member of our church reflects:

> *I find that the less connected I am to people in that place of vulner-
> ability the more my attitudes go back to, you know, just get a job
> [instead of] appreciating someone's struggle in an unjust system.*

1. John Calvin, quoted in Pohl, *Making Room,* 63.
2. Pohl, *Making Room,* 77.
3. Claiborne, "Sharing Economic Resources," 28.

If we entrench ourselves within the dominant society (the "Royal Consciousness"), we will remain separate from the suffering of the least and blinded to the devastation that our cultural practices produce, thus removing any impetus for change and perpetuating the status quo.[4]

> *We are kind of numb. There has been a massive cultural assimilation of people in the church. I think apocalyptic literature is perhaps a lens through which to see our situation, namely that in these apocalyptic writers, the disclosure of the culture and the political and economic system has been monstrous and horrific, thriving off of the death of numerous people in its bid for power and ultimate control. When you have been co-opted you don't see it that way; you see it as kind of benign. There is a myriad of things to be involved in, and I particularly enjoy these things [so] that is what I am going to get involved in. Here is my job, and I want to support myself and my family economically and so we follow the lines of the narrative of the good life that has been laid down in the culture, not recognizing that it has been predicated on massive violence or theft or exploitation. We don't see it as monstrous, we see it as a tame benign thing.*

But as Walter Brueggemann argues in *The Prophetic Imagination*, accompanying those who are suffering can awaken us from this apathy and silence.[5] By taking steps towards sharing the plight of the oppressed and downtrodden, we can become more alert to our captivity to this dominant consciousness that denies or avoids suffering. Brueggemann calls the church to cultivate this "prophetic imagination" and to take up our prophetic task as a church, publicly expressing the suffering and injustice that is so often hidden in our culture so that we can also discover the energizing hope of the God who brings life out of death.[6]

In response to the gospel's call to resist indifference and open our hearts and imaginations to embrace those on the margins, GCBC has developed a considerable number of personal and programmatic responses to the needs of people in our neighborhood, particularly the poor and vulnerable. These practices of hospitality and compassion (works of charity in Catholic nomenclature)—including support for single mothers, tutoring and arts programs for vulnerable children, a weekly meal and shelter

4. Ibid., 32–34.
5. Brueggemann, *Prophetic Imagination*, 46.
6. Ibid., 50.

for the homeless, housing and support services for refugees, the poor and mentally ill—are expressions of the welcome of God we have received in Christ, and they have become central to our identity as a community.

Yet over the last decade, as our church has offered hospitality among the poor and welcomed refugees and immigrants, many people in our church have become increasingly dissatisfied with these "works of charity."

> *I think when you look at these three—charity, advocacy, justice— you see the futility of charity: it is in my mind another form of bond- age. It is just another dependency that becomes just engrained; there does not seem to be any movement from it. For me, giving people things is important on one level, but you are never going to get out of that if you don't go to the justice part.*

This "holy" dissatisfaction deepened as people from more stable life situa- tions and middle-class backgrounds found themselves shifting from help- ing relationships into mutual friendships with those who were poor and vulnerable.

As we sought to advocate on behalf of our new friends, we began to identify the unjust barriers that they were up against. In accompanying refugees, we became aware of lack of advocate support as well as the pain- fully long wait times that refugees often had to endure before their immi- gration hearings. In accompanying those on social assistance, we learned about the many barriers to getting off social assistance and the stigma associated with welfare that makes finding paid employment difficult. Welcoming those who struggle with addictions alerted us to the addictive nature of our society, which has been heightened by the rampant social dislocation and mobility that sever the bonds of community.[7] By hear- ing the stories of First Nations persons, we came to understand why the dominant society wants to keep their story under wraps. By accompany- ing people who were looking for apartments to rent, we encountered the discrimination that people without employment, overcoming addictions, or from a particular ethnic background (particularly Native or Middle Eastern) encountered from landlords, who often refused tenancy to our friends. Through our connections with people from the two-thirds world,

---

7. See Alexander, *Roots of Addiction*. Alexander's essay, in which he studies Native Canadians and Orcadians in Canada, is a convincing argument for rooting the causes of addiction in the severing of social bonds.

we came to identify our own complicity as North Americans in oppressing our global neighbors through the often-unseen impacts of globalization.

And as our eyes were opened to the forces of injustice that plagued our friends, who were simply seeking to live well in the face of poverty, we began to realize that mere acts of charity—giving them a sleeping mat and a hot meal in our church basement once each week or offering them a room in our refugee house—were inadequate.

> *I think that involvement here with Crossroads and Out of the Cold, just over time [led to a] kind of futility or frustration of endlessly feeding more and more people who need shelters and asking the question, why is this happening, and to beginning to look at some of larger social and political, economic trends . . . The thing about the charity and advocacy is that it responds to immediate needs and there needs to be some of that obviously—I mean people are cold or hungry—there needs to be some immediate response, so I am not downplaying that, but if those responses are not done within the larger movements towards justice, then it feels really futile.*

Thus prompted by God's Spirit, who created within our hearts divine anguish and an activist's spirit of protest, we have been stirred from our couches, spurred on by the searing words of the prophet Amos, to grieve and resist the systemic forces of oppression around us and then to seek justice for the least among us.

As we have incorporated corporate confession into our worship more consistently, including a pivotal sermon series on grieving seven years ago that normalized corporate grieving, others have been welcomed into this pursuit, granting a growing freedom within our community to identify and lament the brokenness of our lives and our culture. Some of the most powerful expressions of our brokenness have been the contemporary Stations of the Cross created by artists in our church each year during Lent.[8] Our recent public lament held at various points along Commercial Drive (the main strip near our church) invited bystanders to join us in a liturgy of confession around such issues of injustice such as trafficking of women and homelessness.

8. On the power of symbols to reveal social injustice and incite social change, see Bruggemann, *Prophetic Imagination,* 39–40.

FROM BLAME TOWARDS COMPASSIONATE ACTION

Shortly after Out of the Cold (our church's hot meal and overnight program) began, I told the story of Dixie in a sermon I gave from the text in Amos 5.

> *Dixie, one of the squeegee guys who comes to Out of the Cold, told me how he left a non-existent family in Nova Scotia to come here. After two years of rejections and closed doors from job hunting, he gave up on finding a real job here in Vancouver. Dixie feels like he has no hope left of finding a steady job and that working as a squeegee washer is at least an attempt at working to make a living and to retain a little dignity, despite the fact that a lot of people swear at him or even spit at him when they see him. So what do you say to Dixie? Do you say what I heard two men standing on the corner of Commercial "Get a job, you god-damned kid." Ironically, Dixie told me that he feels condemned already. It's not so easy for Dixie to solve his problems. Some of you know how hard it can be to find a job today. I'm sure there are some people here today who have been looking for work or for a better job for longer than Dixie. If you can't find work, does that mean that you are condemned, that you are doing something wrong to deserve this?*

Stories like Dixie's compelled us to investigate issues around unemployment, and we found some seed money for a woman in our congregation with a community development and business background to do a study interviewing unemployed or underemployed folks in our congregation so that she could identify the barriers to employment that they faced and propose some potential responses we could make.[9] D.'s findings confirmed the barriers people face in seeking employment. One refugee spoke of the barriers to employment with Canadian work experience: "*How do you even make up a resume if you don't have work experience?*"[10] Another spoke of personal barriers: "*I have an anxiety disorder; I get afraid and then won't go to work because I am afraid.*"[11] Some of the interviewees expressed disappointment that the church had not been more intentional in helping the unemployed find work: "*I didn't find anyone in this church*

9. Randall, "Research on Economic Needs and Development Opportunities."

10. Ibid., 9.

11. Ibid., 7.

who said '*I have a job for you.*'"[12] I wonder how many poor folk receive this response in our churches.

Prompted by the desire to assist those who were without work in finding employment, a small group of church members launched JustWork, an economic development initiative that linked worksites, vocational counseling and small business coaching. After a couple years of limited success in finding people jobs and helping people start businesses, we shifted our focus to developing social enterprises.

> We believe that the top priority for JustWork is developing social enterprises. Once we have established social enterprises, then we can better fulfill our vision by inviting people from the business sector to see (hands on) another way of providing employment. We can help people develop work skills, people skills and vocational direction by inviting those who need these skills into the social enterprises. We can also begin to offer education for the larger community, offering a wider vision of what work is.

Two factors influenced our shift in this direction: an awareness that people who were successful in finding work by enrolling in employment programs were likely to find employment eventually, with or without that program; and a recognition that people who had barriers, due to alcohol or drug addictions or mental illnesses, were very unlikely to maintain employment, even if they secured a job. Social enterprises allowed people to find a work environment that fit them, whether that was piecework with a flexible schedule or part-time work with an empathetic supervisor.

The other factor that led us towards developing social enterprises was the already existing pottery studio in the basement of our church. The "potter's house," begun by two potters from our church a couple years earlier, had become a place of welcome for many people in our neighborhood.

> The Potter's House welcomes people from the neighborhood who would otherwise not have access to a creative studio space, due to economic or social barriers. The studio provides studio space, instruction, support and employment opportunities through pottery making. The studio is committed to: community building, acceptance, creativity, healing, and dignity.[13]

12. Ibid., 15.

13. Online: http://gcbchurch.ca under "community presence."

With that base of connections and community, we launched JustPotters, a social enterprise that empowers people with barriers to employment in the "regular workforce" to do piecework or develop their own pottery for sale, offering training and support along the way. The studio has launched a number of people into a vocation in pottery and created a community of care and healing. One person, after returning from her yearly retreat, declared to me that she had "found a place to truly belong." Especially hopeful has been seeing one of the participants, a long-time neighbor, proceed from her role as a participant towards an experience of healing in her own life towards becoming the new manager. With a compassion borne out of her own experience of poverty and chaos, she demonstrates remarkable empathy for those with whom she works in the studio.

A year later, JustWork launched JustGarden, an enterprise that shared common commitments with JustPotters:

> As an organic landscape gardening company, JustGarden provides meaningful work as gardeners to people with barriers to employment. Working with a small group of people on a long-term basis, JustGarden stewards creation as it stewards relationships and the gift of work.[14]

Our manager, who has both chaplaincy training and landscaping experience, employs people for shorter shifts, giving them opportunities to gain work and life skills as well as opportunities for increased employment. Some of these employees, especially refugee claimants who required Canadian work experience, have found full-time landscaping jobs elsewhere. Others have gained a sense of dignity from meaningful work and pay that supplements their social-service benefits. Many homeowners who employ JustGarden have indicated that they chose us because of quality results and their desire to contribute to social good.

JustCatering, the third enterprise launched by JustWork, was formed by T., who with her husband opens their home for meals and friendship with those on the street. The trust she has already established with these friends has motivated them to do their work well and to contribute back some of the hospitality that they themselves have received.

14. Ibid.

As JustWork seeks to develop more social enterprises, they hope to develop their mandate of stimulating existing business to alter their employment practices to include those who might not fit into existing conceptions of "a good employee." They have begun to take up this aspect of their vision by welcoming employers to observe their social enterprises and by speaking to business owners and managers directly, encouraging them to consider their social responsibility to provide meaningful work that brings dignity (and financial benefit) to those who are marginalized or excluded from the workplace. In this effort, JustWork hopes to alter the landscape, not only of gardens, but also of work environments throughout the city.

One advisory member of JustWork comments about our need to awaken to the injustices in our economic system.

> I think JustWork moved from seeing people that were unemployed and giving them money—I don't know if our church was involved in that, not since I've been here, but lots of churches seem to do that as their response to unemployment, to provide charity—I think where we are moving in JustWork is beyond advocacy to focusing not only on people who are unemployed, but starting to say what is wrong with the system, why some people have jobs and some people don't, and seeing the problem as being not just these people that can't find work, but the whole system that doesn't allow, doesn't enable people to have meaningful work, or dignified work. So I think JustWork is moving in that direction, seeking justice and transformation on a broader level.

Towards Seeking Justice for the Least

Whereas the majority of our congregation has readily accepted the first two trajectories as consistent with the gospel,[15] it has taken more time for our congregation to embrace this third trajectory, in part because of the entrenched dualism in North American Christianity between our spiritu-

---

15. This is true in theory although not always in practice, as we discover the cost and sacrifices involved in moving further along these trajectories. Given that we are continually incorporating new people into our church, this is not surprising. One of the questions I will explore below is how we can be more intentional about marking these paths and helping people take up these practices.

ality/theology and our socio-political/economic life.[16] The acceptance of this dualism has made many people within our congregation suspicious about the church's involvement in justice issues. Yet the biblical narrative cannot be divorced from seeking justice for the least, for as Gustavo Gutierrez writes: "To know Yahweh, which in Biblical language is equivalent to saying to love Yahweh, is to establish just relationships among men; it is to recognize the right of the poor."[17]

As Nicholas Wolterstorff explains in the description of his own evolution of the concept of justice, this biblical call to seek justice for the least is not first about punishment:

> Slowly I began to see that the Bible is a book about justice, but what a strange and haunting form of justice! Not our familiar modern Western justice, of no one invading your right to determine your life as you will. Rather, it is the justice of the widow, the orphan and the alien. A society is just when all the little ones, all the defenseless ones, all the unprotected ones have been brought back into community, to enjoy a fair share in the community's goods and a standing and voice in the affairs of the community.[18]

Similarly, Deuteronomy affirms this view of justice: "You shall not pervert the justice due an alien or an orphan, nor take a widow's garment in pledge."[19] The prophets take the Jewish people to task for ignoring justice, affirming the call of God's people to "let justice roll on like a river."[20] Jesus' death and resurrection shapes both our understanding of justice and the *modus operandi* for pursuing it in the world. God acts in and through Jesus to deliver us from captivity to the powers that misshape our world, both the human expressions and the spiritual realities that lie behind them. God restores these powers to their divinely created and ordered purposes.[21] The church then is called to proclaim this vision of a

---

16. Newbigin, *Foolishness to the Greeks*, 4–22.

17. Gutierrez, *Theology of Liberation*, 195.

18. Wolterstorff, "Grace That Shaped My Life," 273. See also his two books devoted to this theme, *Until Justice and Peace Embrace* and *Justice*.

19. Deut 24:17.

20. E.g. Amos 5:24 and Micah 6:8.

21. Wright, *Surprised by Hope*, 213–21. See also Newbigin, *Gospel in a Pluralist Society*, 200–210, where he discusses these principalities and powers, arguing that Christ came not to destroy but to disarm and redirect these powers towards the life of the kingdom.

renewed creation, where justice and peace can flourish, both by holding the powers of rulers and authorities accountable to their true purpose and by bearing witness in their communal life and involvements in society to the Bible's vision of *Shalom.*

This biblical framework for the work of justice-seeking brings clarity to the old debates about the tension between evangelism and social justice, for Jesus' victory over the powers engenders both our proclamation of this truth as well as our embodiment of the restored way of life towards which Jesus' resurrection moves us.[22] One of our resident academic theologians articulates well how this view of justice might look in our culture:

> *Justice is about ensuring mutual dignity and honour, sharing resources for sustaining and nurturing life and health, and meaningfully participating in the processes of social and political decision-making. It entails the establishment of regulations that ensure adequate care and sustenance for the most vulnerable and limiting the acquisition of power and possessions, so that the community's resources are not concentrated in the hands of a few, while many go without. This means that particular attention is given to those who lack these social and material goods. A just society, therefore, would be one in which wealth and power were more or less evenly distributed, where gross inequalities of resources are not sanctioned and opportunities for participation are nurtured.*[23]

The desire to integrate spirituality and justice has become more evident in both the preaching and dialogue within our congregation. One congregant identifies the revitalizing impulse for faithful living that our movement along this trajectory has brought into all areas of our lives:

22. Newbigin, *Gospel in a Pluralist Society*, 270. See also 136: "What is true in the affirmation of the Evangelical side of this debate is that it does matter supremely that every human being should have the opportunity to know Jesus as Lord and Saviour, that without a living Church where this witness is borne, neither evangelism nor Christian social action is possible, and that the gospel can never be identified with any particular project for justice and peace however laudable and promising. What is true in the position of the social activists is that a Church which exists only for itself and its own enlargement is a witness against the gospel, that the Church exists not for itself and not for its members but as a sign and agent and foretaste of the kingdom of God, and that it is impossible to give faithful witness to the gospel while being indifferent to the situation of the hungry, the sick, the victims of human inhumanity."

23. Diewert interview in *Clarion: Journal of Spirituality and Justice.*

It is refreshing that the gospel is seen as more than just the means of a personal salvation or some form of spiritual experience that we are called to be a part of but recognizing that it has broader implications beyond just a personal level: the gospel means something in the world we live in, not just me being in a right relationship with God, which is of course important, but it also has this notion of being in right relationship with our neighbors and families and acting in such a way to see the justice of God brought into those contexts.

But if we are going to pursue a more just society and search for creative ways to respond to structural and systemic wrongs, we cannot remain in isolation as a church, but will need to work cooperatively with other churches and neighborhood groups. As Shane Claiborne suggests, we don't need new churches as much as we need the church to work together for the good of the city.[24]

Our response to issues around housing and homelessness took a step outward, drawing in people beyond our church, when a couple from our church established "Streams of Justice," an inter-church activist group that has attracted people from diverse churches in Vancouver, as well as those with no church connection or background at all. Through insightful analysis of our culture and provocative biblical teaching, Streams of Justice seeks to confront injustice and prompt the community to take collective action towards a more just city in the biblical tradition of that word.

Starting that series of Monday night courses and then realizing that we can't go on just offering the series of full courses on describing the problem or try to awaken the sort of awareness biblically and socially in our current context without engaging more sustained efforts on this front. So Streams of Justice emerged out of that need for praxis, for action that follows upon our analysis and reflection. To engage in those together—both the practice, reflection, or the analysis and the action—that is how we got launched. I wanted to do it within the context of the church, Christianity, because I felt like there is some real potential here. There is a real need to awaken that in people and to develop educational strategies, communication strategies as well as initiatives of action.

So far, this group has taken action around such issues of homelessness and poverty (in part related to the Olympics), exploitation of ab-

---

24. Claiborne, *Irresistible Revolution*, 144–45.

originals, the war on drugs, and prostitution.[25] Their recent creative arts presentation, "Being poor in a world-class city," shed light upon the way our city is prone to view poverty as a blight on our beautiful surroundings, leading our politicians and public to criminalize the poorest among us.

But there are powerful forces in our culture that try to divert our community away from this call to seek justice for the least, and there are also immense challenges for those sustaining this prophetic vision among us.[26]

> *I feel like this is our role—to point out the systemic injustice and to try to change that . . . I don't know how to do it and it feels really slow and I can't imagine my involvement in seeking justice and seeking any change in the system is going to have a huge impact. It feels really hopeless but it is like—what else can you do? That is where I am at.*

The pursuit of justice has also been taken by one of the Asian members of our congregation. In an article in B. C. Christian News, B. tells his story of meeting a disheveled native man on the street, buying him a meal and listening to his story. *"Without knowledge of the First People's history and struggle then, I found his story very foreign . . . Little did I know then that after centuries of injustice, the First People have no wish to be immigrants in their own land."*[27] When B. shared "the gospel" with him, as he

25. See more about their actions and analysis online: www.streamsofjustice.org.

26. D.'s story has raised some fascinating discussion reflecting differing cultural perspectives and the challenge of understanding one another. When D., a teacher at a respected theological academy, gave up his teaching position without knowing what lay ahead but wanting to spend more time in the neighborhood, some of our church celebrated this decision as the call of the gospel towards downward mobility while others, particularly those immigrants or refugees who were working at low-paying service jobs to give their children a better life, were befuddled why someone would leave a good job and what he had been trained to do, now having no way to financially support his family. Rice discusses this sort of phenomenon when he writes about the community home in which he lived where black and white folks together sought to care for their poor neighbors. "Spencer's theory was that educated whites who came from family histories of social privilege, and had come to see the dead end of materialism and the 'rat race,' were now willing to mobilize downward. But African American life was on a very different trajectory, coming from the margins into new educational and economic possibilities, mobilizing upward" ("Lamenting Racial Divisions," 65). This same sort of reality exists in our church.

27. Chu, "Abandoned Dinner."

understood it at the time, the man bolted from his meal, yelling at B., "You are one of them." This rejection, along with the experience of organizing an impromptu prayer meeting attended by over six thousand for the victims of the Tiananmen square massacre, led B. into a discovery of the call of the kingdom for justice and peace. "*In my own search afterwards, the whole aspect of the kingdom of God became clear as the real foundation for why we are doing what we are doing.*"

After these experiences, B. began devoting himself to a vocation of justice-seeking, by raising the profile of kingdom theology in churches, especially Chinese churches, and by diving headlong into some specific issues of injustice. Shortly after joining our congregation, B. organized a series of truth and reconciliation events at our church, wherein he invited some of the considerable friends he had made in the aboriginal community to tell their stories of loss and pain. He also arranged a number of group bus trips to Mount Currie reserve so that people could see the conditions people lived under and dialogue with the people directly. These encounters culminated in a "March for Reconciliation" in which over thirty-five people from our church participated in a summons to our city to settle ongoing disputes with First Nations bands in the name of the gospel of reconciliation. A couple of years later, B., along with a woman from our church with a two-decade history of work in the native community, organized a banquet attended by nearly five hundred people, where Chinese immigrants and Aboriginal folk shared common stories of struggle and hope. These issues continue to have attention drawn to them through the now annual parade and related events with First Nations and Chinese Christians on Chinese New Year.

Reconciliation between native and non-native British Columbians is only one issue B. has taken up and in which he has been able to involve others. He organized local opposition to gambling expansion at our local exhibition grounds, exposed the government's failure to remove from sale fish imported from China which had unacceptable toxicity levels, and has spoken out publicly regarding a number of public concerns, in all of which he has drawn people from our church to be involved.

One of B.'s strengths is his refusal to be co-opted by partisan politics, continuing to take on issues traditionally associated with both the right and the left on the political spectrum. B. has done well at allowing the gospel of the kingdom to critique evil opposed to, and affirm truth consistent with, this kingdom vision, wherever it is found. B. comments on this tendency of churches to be co-opted into "*the extreme right or the extreme left too. In the absence of the true kingdom of God, in looking at what it should be, one can easily fall into a more leftist type of view of life and take it at that.*" The church has sought to follow the same route through partisan politics, sometimes more successfully than others. One of the challenges has been to continually articulate how the kingdom vision is alternative in some aspects to many of the political options currently on offer, while at the same time encouraging people to get involved publicly and take concrete actions. Sticking close to the biblical vision can provide the resources for this narrow path, as Wright contends: "If you push the Bible off the table you are merely colluding with the pagan empire, denying yourself the sourcebook for your kingdom critique of oppression."[28]

One other group that B. organized a couple of years ago, "Faith Communities Called to Solidarity With the Poor," brought over ten different denominations and churches together in response to the permit that the city of Vancouver required another church to secure in order to continue to operate its own Out of the Cold meal. Three press conferences and two meetings with the city later, this group has, we hope, convinced the city not to require churches to seek permits to carry out an act that is intrinsic to its purpose, caring for the least among us. So far, the group has elicited nearly three thousand signatures on petition opposing this permit requirement, thereby also elevating the call to solidarity with the poor among churches that are less familiar with this characteristic of the kingdom. This effort has occupied a lot of time and effort for three of us from our church, and yet it has given opportunity to bear witness to the city. The effort has challenged their narrow definitions of worship, which seek to limit the activities of churches, and promoted the point that Christian worship is intertwined with care for the poor, or perhaps more succinctly, that care for the poor is part of Christian worship. Recently, the Mayor tabled a motion to widen the definition of worship and withdraw the permit requirement.

But moving along this trajectory of seeking justice for the least requires a certain persistence over time in order to delve deeply enough into

28. Wright, *Surprised by Hope*, 219.

the concrete realities of these structural issues and discern how to respond to them. *"So, I feel like the resistance and the struggle to imagine otherwise is a right one and a noble one even if it feels like . . . you are fighting the long defeat."*

For example, the lack of affordable housing in our neighborhood has led us—through a discernment process that has evolved over two decades—to four different levels of responses: 1) crisis/emergency response; 2) personal response; 3) communal response; 4) systemic response. These four levels of response reflect our attempt to address this social issue systemically and holistically.

In order to extend the welcome of God to those who are in immediate crisis and at the most risk, we open our church building on Thursday, Friday, and Saturday nights for the six coldest months of the year. While essential for the well-being of these homeless folk, this "level one" response alone is not only inadequate, but may perpetuate the crisis by allowing society and government—at federal, provincial, civic, and community levels—to ignore the problem.

By opening our community houses to those who are homeless or at risk of homelessness, we not only improve affordability for all those in the house by lowering rental costs, we also share in the life of community together as a sign of God's restoring and welcoming presence among us. This "level two" response is an act of resistance to society's apathy towards homeless people, as Pohl suggests:

> People view hospitality as quaint and tame partly because they do not understand the power of recognition. When a person who is not valued by society is received by a socially respected person or group as a human being with dignity and worth, small transformations occur. The person's self-assessment, so often tied to societal assessment, is enhanced. Because such actions are counter-cultural, they are a witness to the larger community, which is then challenged to reassess its standards and methods of valuing. Many persons who are not valued by the larger community are essentially invisible to it. When people are socially invisible, their needs and concerns are not acknowledged and no one even notices the injustices they suffer.[29]

---

29. Pohl, *Making Room*, 61. This same power of recognition has been transformative in our partnership with Urban Promise, who run summer day camps and after-school

A resident in one of our community houses concurs: "*Radical hospitality is actually a form of justice because it is confronting the dominant culture and the powers and the systems and structures. When we blur the lines of host and those who are welcomed, that moves us from just charity toward justice.*"

Recently, the church made the decision to work with our partner organization, Salsbury Community Society, to build around twenty units of social housing with an accompanying ten units of a new monastic community over top underground parking. Because current by-laws have changed to allow social housing without providing parking (since most residents don't own a vehicle), we are able to build social housing at a considerably lower cost by donating the land for the project (and still maintaining church parking underground).[30] By taking corporate/communal action (a "level three" response) towards constructing social housing, our church is seeking to use our physical assets for the common good *Wow /*

Given that the welfare rates for housing allowance remained static from 1994 to 2006, it is hardly surprising that homelessness skyrocketed during that same period. Judy Graves, the city's housing coordinator, reminded the participants at a housing conference that income, housing and support are the three ingredients required for truly helping homeless people. To that end, some from our congregation participated in the "Raise the Rates" campaign (a "level four" systemic response), a coalition of groups seeking to compel our provincial government to raise welfare allowances to livable amounts. Another group from our congregation held a squat (a week-long occupancy) on an empty lot devoted to new social housing, but which had sat dormant for over three years, awaiting action by the provincial government. They also initiated a week-long vigil

---

tutoring at our church. By making their program accessible to the poorer children in the neighborhood, and by welcoming teens as street leaders who might not otherwise have jobs or organized activities during these months, Urban Promise has granted greater value to these young people. Watching them grow in self-esteem and self-evaluation has been delightful.

30. At a recent housing conference, I pitched this idea as one potential means of putting a dent in the homeless situation across the Vancouver region. So far, one city council in a neighboring city, Abbotsford, informed me that this idea has been taken seriously in their strategy discussion regarding homelessness.

in front of our city hall to bring attention to the lack of action on promises made by Council.

While not everyone in the church (or neighborhood) embraces all of these responses, the presence of those who are taking these actions has expanded the imagination of those who are new to the church or who had never considered participating in these ways. In this way, the church has become a discipling community of the sort reflected in Paul's words to the Philippians: "Brothers and sisters, join in imitating me, and observe those who live according to the example you have in us."[31]

Our unchurched neighbors have also been drawn into the vortex of this transformation. When Crossroads (the group that hosts our Out of the Cold program) attempted to relocate to the house adjacent to the church building, our immediate neighbors resisted this move by starting a petition. The Crossroads advisory committee responded by hosting a dialogue in the church basement, where residents were invited to share their fears about homeless people walking into their backyards and stealing stuff or taking up too much space on a street already crowded with pedestrian traffic. Residents who were part of the church empathized with their neighbors' concerns, but also talked about how knowing the folks from Out of the Cold had reduced alienation and fear and increased their trust as they saw their new friends extend care and a watchful presence to the neighborhood. The guests of Out of the Cold spoke passionately about their desire to respect people's property since they now felt like valued members of the community. Over the course of the evening, while some of the residents continued to resist the relocation of Crossroads, others supported the move, some offered to volunteer, and some began to offer plums to one of our community houses. Through this dialogue, many of the residents opened their hearts to their homeless neighbors, the nameless people whom they'd feared when they walked into the church hall that evening.

The evolution from charity to advocacy to seeking justice for the least has also marked the journey of Kinbrace, our neighborhood house for refugee claimants. From simply providing a house of "charity" to refugee claimants, to advocating on their behalf in order to access services, to accompanying them through the complicated permanent residency

---

31. Phil 3:17.

application process, those involved with Kinbrace have been moved over the last decade to address the structural and systemic issues that prevent refugees from finding security and stability here in Canada.

The presence of many of the Kinbrace refugees within our church congregation has alerted all of us to issues of global injustice (such as the history of colonization, globalization, the wealth gap between the North and South, inter-tribal warfare, religious persecution), as we have heard stories of Oromo persecution in Ethiopia, entrenched poverty in Bolivia, El Salvador's history of war and disappearances and China's suffering church, as well as stories of great courage, beauty and faithfulness amidst hardships in all these situations. These stories have motivated some in our church to join with groups seeking to bring systemic change in these countries and also to ask how we might live more justly in our own countries of residence and/or origin.

REED (Resist Exploitation and Embrace Dignity) is one such justice-seeking initiative that emerged within our congregation. With the relative lack of resources in Canada for responding to human trafficking, REED "stands against trafficking and sexual exploitation through incarnational outreach, prophetic advocacy and transformational education."[32] M., REED's founder, offers assistance to women who are being exploited by trafficking, raises awareness among the wider church community regarding the prevalence of the international trafficking of women in the sex trade, and also counsels politicians and police officers around issues of law enforcement and legislation.

Given that environmental impact is one of the most significant justice issues that humankind has ever faced,[33] many of GCBC's congregants have sought to live out the biblical mandate to steward creation in our urban context by planting and tending community gardens, often in places that have been more or less ignored or abandoned, such as abandoned housing lots, unkempt boulevards and vacant yards. These gardens have not only supplied food for homeless friends, but have also been a context for building community and nurturing beauty in places of ugliness. Symbolic gestures, even diminutive gestures like these gardens, give

32. Online at http://embracedignity.wordpress.com, which offers a description of their most recent efforts.

33. Reiher, "Creation, Justice and the Holy Spirit," in Catford, *Following Fire*, 308.

public expression to this alternative world of Shalom, thereby prompting the whole neighborhood to dream together of a different future.[34] In this world of Shalom, justice and delight go hand-in-hand.[35]

Justice at Work

One of the temptations in a church like ours with so many programmatic responses to seeking justice requiring many volunteers is to focus our attention on these and underemphasize the importance of living justly in our workplaces, the locations where many people spend the majority of their time and energy.

In response to this lack, we preached and studied in our home groups through a series entitled "Faith at Work" where we spent at least fifteen minutes each Sunday during our worship services interviewing people about how their faith affected their work. Participants included two actors, two geologists, one car-lot employee, an anesthetist, two teachers, two people who worked in mental health, one construction manager, and one unemployed volunteer. The stories of these folk revealed some of the pressures people were under: geologists grappling with the tensions between their role as stewards and the coercion of company executives to ignore environmental concerns; a construction manager who worked seventy hours per week on a regular basis to meet deadlines; an actress who worked at low-paying service jobs to pursue her vocation in the theater; a medical specialist who spoke of the subtle pressures to uphold the social hierarchies in hospitals by ignoring janitors or nurses' aids; a teacher who encountered high school students unconcerned with the common good. (These interviewees, especially the car-lot employee, also expressed gratitude for their jobs and the opportunity to use their skills in their paid work.) During the preaching we sought to name the powers that impact our work, including the all-encompassing nature of much employment,

34. Mike Roberts, a Vancouver Province columnist, gave greater exposure to the peace garden when he wrote an article about it. The Province also wrote an article about the garden begun by T. W. in the Downtown Eastside. The coverage by local media gives credence to the symbolic power of these gardens.

35. See Wolterstorff, *Until Justice and Peace Embrace*, 124–40 wherein he lays out the vision of a city of delight. He argues convincingly that justice calls for liberation from evil *and* the cultivation of beauty and delight.

the status-seeking attached to some jobs, the futility of many tasks, inter-employee conflict and the pervasive influence of the bottom line as the only evaluation of paid work.

After we finished this series, a woman who views her primary vo-cation as her paid medical work told me that she felt *"like a part of the church"* after this series. The series accentuated our need to make continu-ing strides to resource people theologically in their employment. Thinking theologically about how to engage our work in ways that plant seeds of the kingdom reflects the truth that seeking justice is not a peripheral activity for those who are interested in justice issues but a way of being in the world.

> The practice of prophetic ministry is not some special thing done two days a week. Rather, it is done in, with, and under all the acts of ministry—it concerns a stance and posture or a hermeneutic about the world of death and the word of life that can be brought to light in every context.[36]

If we are to take up this stance, we will need to reflect on how the current shape of market capitalism (mis)shapes our desire. Building on the insights of Gilles Deleuze, Daniel Bell comments about how the mar-ket's force becomes all-pervasive in shaping our desire:

> The capitalist machine deterritorializes desire: it overruns all pre-vious social formations and releases the flows of desire that these formations had organized and regulated. The capitalist machine also reterritorializes desire: it subjects desire to the axiomatic of production for the market.[37]

---

36. Brueggemann, *Prophetic Imagination,* 111. Phillip D. Kenneson gives an example of how powerfully a movement to live differently in everyday life can lead to an alterna-tive society: "If Christians lobby Congress to restrict the amount of violence on televi-sion, this is considered 'real political action.' If Christians put their television sets in the closet, however, this is considered a private matter, a personal lifestyle choice, a simple apolitical preference. But certainly if all people who regard themselves as Christian did the latter, it would have a sizable impact on the social order we call the United States of America. Isn't such ordering of the social the traditional concern of politics?" (Kenneson, *Life on the Vine,* 51).

37. Bell, *Liberation Theology After the End of History,* 19.

Bell believes that the Church can reterritorialize desire for the kingdom if we faithfully take up the gamut of practices arising from the gospel.[38] The sermon series was an initial attempt to shape our own desires for the kingdom by taking up the practice of seeking to implement God's vision of justice in our workplaces.

I shared one story in the final sermon in the series that conveys the possibility of doing just that:

> I once interviewed here in our worship a fellow named Sam, who was part of our church a decade or so ago. Sam spoke about his work at a fish packing plant where he was the biologist responsible to decide if the fish had too many toxins to feed to humans. He talked about how stressful that work was and the pressure he got from the company to let the fish through, regardless if the toxicity levels were dangerous to human health. We prayed for Sam that day. One year later, someone came up to him and told him that·they had continued to pray for him that entire year. Sam told me what a difference those prayers made in his life and work. He felt that God was there with him, that he was somehow doing his work for and before God. "Do your work with enthusiasm, as the Lord and not to men and women, knowing that whatever good we do, we will receive the same again from the Lord, whether we are slaves or free."[39]

The Whole with the Parts

> [The church's vision] is broad. It's not just about ministering to Christians and developing programs just for ourselves. We are very aware of looking outward to the neighborhood, social justice, compassion, solidarity with the poor, all those things which have come up. Not just those things that the media picks up on but individual, personal stories, too.

One of the vital characteristics of this unfolding mission of GCBC has been the way in which the many and various parts fit into the whole, or how the different responses, ministries, community houses, justice-seeking efforts and healing prayers fit together as a joint venture aimed towards a vision of the kingdom of God among us. By belonging to the

---

38. Ibid., 87–100. I will return to this theme, the shaping of desire, in my conclusion.

39. The reference is found in Eph 5:7–8.

larger community and vision, each venture has been strengthened and empowered to take more risks in resisting and standing against the cultural forces that dehumanize us. For example, while M.'s primary vocation is to resist the exploitation of women in the sex trade, she finds strength knowing that other people in her community are working to help single mothers escape poverty and avoid the desperation and isolation that might lead them into the sex trade. In some ways, this is similar to the base ecclesial communities in Latin America, which work with the poor and vulnerable, yet remain connected to the Catholic Church for worship and encouragement.[40]

Moreover, by belonging to a larger whole, the individuals involved in the various programs and ministries that have emerged from GCBC have been empowered to resist atomizing forces and to find our way through transitions and conflicts. Without this communal effort, it would be easy to give up working for social change and instead search for "individual, biographical solutions to systemic contradictions."[41] For example, when one of our community houses had an exodus of three of the five women living there in a three-month span, there were others from the community ready to move in and renew the vision for that house as a place of welcome. Rather than the house disbanding with a sense of failure and guilt—what we have seen happen in some other isolated community living ventures in our city—belonging to a larger community allowed these folks to move on in freedom, and the house was retained for community living as new people emerged who shared this common vision.

This inter-connectedness has also given newcomers an opportunity to observe how others are taking up these practices, gaining a realistic idea of what it would mean for them to take a further step along a trajectory. For example, someone who had never participated in a protest got to know another person from the church who was organizing an effort to bring public attention to homelessness. When the organizer invited that person to participate, he joined in partly because he knew and trusted the organizer.

40. Leonardo Boff discusses this cooperative structure in *Saint Francis*, 119–27.
41. Bauman, *Society Under Siege*, 195.

But if we are to retain the strengths that emerge as parts find their connection to the larger community, we will need leadership that empowers people to live out this vision of the kingdom.

> *You sort of come at things sideways and something moves forward incrementally and then moves sideways, and then it starts moving forward again. And so I think the first thing that comes to mind (and the word is used a lot) is the organic nature of things. You have to learn how to lead in a way that continually comes back and pulls all the pieces together and steps forward and back and forward and around and sideways and forward.*

Charity and Justice Together

> We are building a world in which persons are more important than things and in which all can live with dignity.[42]

A kingdom community is one where the rich and poor come together in the name of Christ, a community where the transforming power of the gospel touches all, where both rich and poor are summoned to personal responsibility for our actions.

> We try to hold in tension personal responsibility for both the rich and the poor as well as systemic factors leading to differences in the look of their conversions. The conversion of both to the heart and purposes of God has interesting and challenging implications. For the powerful, conversion involves moving into the purposes of God in caring for and in repentance regarding the poor. For the poor, conversion involves empowerment and forgiveness to oppressors.[43]

Charity without justice can perpetuate the status quo and become an idol. On the other hand, justice without a community that practices works of charity can lead to the sort of angry self-righteousness that characterizes so much activism in our world. Seeking justice while involved in works of charity sinks us into the personal stories of people, calling forth and rooting our actions in love.

---

42. Gutierrez, *We Drink from our Own Wells*, 27.
43. Ringma, "Liberation Theologians Speak to Evangelicals," 7.

> *I have a friend who will get involved in seeking justice on larger*
> *scales, for example, in political action, but she may not be involved*
> *at the personal level with anyone. That's too challenging [for her].*
> *It's easier to go to a demonstration and get arrested than to have*
> *someone who is needing your care and being available to give that*
> *care.*[44]

Seeking justice can be a way "to love more than one person at a time."[45] Indeed, this perspective reflects God's own character and vision for humanity, as expressed in the stirring metaphor from Psalm 85: "Steadfast love and faithfulness will meet, justice and peace will kiss each other."

As we seek justice for the least as a church, we will need to provide an ecclesiology that empowers us to dialogue about justice issues in a way that leads to action, even if we don't all agree. Otherwise, our differences around socio-political issues may lead to non-action or neutrality, since we might fear that taking a stand will divide us. But if we are to persist in pursuing this trajectory, we will need to face our own idolatries and move further into the love of God.

44. Of course, anger and love can co-exist in harmony when anger arises from love and is without sin, as in the character of God (cf. Heb 12:5–11).

45. I first heard this line from Rebecca Pippert years ago in one of her talks.

SEVEN

Navigating the Rapids of our Idolatries

There is such a thing as idolatry and we must guard against it.
Indeed, we must put it to death without pity.[1]

As the people of GCBC have sought to take up the practices of radical hospitality, integrated multicultural living, and seeking justice for the least, we have come up against idolatrous forces in ourselves and in our culture. These idolatries might inhibit us from taking the next steps in obedience to God or tempt us to value something or someone in a way that hinders the love and trust we owe to God. As Wright contends, "with the entire Jewish tradition, the basic sin is idolatry, the worship of that which is not in fact the living Creator God."[2] Human desire, deep and restless and seemingly unfulfillable, keeps stuffing itself with finite goods, but these cannot satisfy. If we try to fill our hearts with anything besides the God of the universe, we will become overfed but undernourished, and day by day, week by week, year after year, we will be thinned down to a mere outline of a human being.[3]

> Idolatry is always the perversion of something good. Greed—
> worshipping the appetites and what they feed on—is the perver-
> sion of the God-given instinct for the proper enjoyment of the
> good creation. The proper response to idolatry is therefore not

1. Wright, *Surprised By Hope*, 212.
2. Wright, *Paul*, 35.
3. Plantinga, *Not The Way It's Supposed To Be*, 122–23.

dualism, the rejection of space, time or matter as themselves evil
or dangerous, but the renewed worship of the Creator God, which
sets the context for the proper enjoyment and use of the created
order without the danger of worshipping it.[4]

But by seeking to welcome rather than exclude, to value one another
in our differences rather than hold one other apart in suspicion, to seek
justice for the least rather than our own security and health, we collide
with these objects of false worship, and we are confronted with the same
choice that the people of Israel faced in the desert: will we worship God,
or will we worship idols?[5]

TOWARDS CONFESSION AND REPENTANCE

Liberation of society comes not from those who try to change
society, but from those who try to be their true selves.[6]

Through the practice of confession, we come to recognize and name—before God and one another—some of the robust forces that misshape our
lives and society. Through the practice of repentance, we turn away from
these forces, towards a merciful God, trusting in the power of the Holy
Spirit to transform us and escort us towards new life in Christ. Ronald
Rolheiser describes this cycle of repentance—our death to loss and sin
and subsequent resurrection to new life in Christ—as the "pattern of the
paschal mystery,"[7] because this path of liberation follows the way of the
cross. Our deepening participation in the kingdom of God depends upon
our persistence in this turn.

The church is never more in danger than when it sees itself simply
as the solution-bearer and forgets that every day it too must say
"Lord, have mercy on me, a sinner," and allow that confession to

4. Wright, *Surprised by Hope*, 212.

5. Exod 20:2–5: "I am the Lord, your God, who brought you out of the land of Egypt,
out of the house of slavery; you shall have no other gods before me. You shall not make
for yourself an idol . . . you shall not bow down or worship them."

6. Palmer, *Let Your Life Speak*, 49.

7. Rolheiser, *Holy Longing*, 141–66.

work its way into genuine humility even as it stands boldly before
the world and its crazy empires.[8]

In traveling along this trajectory of repentance and confession, we are
following a pathway familiar to the church in its two millennia of history,[9]
but it is one marked by footprints unique to our own context and culture.

> *I think the whole matter of confession and repentance has been
> flipped upside down or inside out. Whereas before it meant expos-
> ing or becoming vulnerable, with the chance of being hurt, repen-
> tance has changed to becoming a tool of faith which enables me
> to live here in this place and in this time and with this people. So
> confession has become a tool I can use in order to receive the love
> of God and the fellowship of God's Spirit with me in ways that I
> haven't been able to experience before. So that has moved me into a
> deeper life with God. It has become the way to being strengthened.
> Paul talks about the inner core being strengthened in order for the
> kingdom to come near.*

Over the past two decades, the practice of confession and repentance
within our congregation has developed and matured. Rather than being
part of our corporate worship, our focus at the beginning was on the initial act of repentance at conversion. But after a sermon series in 1994 that
named confession and repentance as a major part of Jesus' preaching, in
which we noticed the prominent warnings about idolatry held in Jesus'
itinerant preaching, we began to include confession as a more regular element in our worship.[10] Five years ago, after a presentation to our worship
teams on the movements of worship, the confession of our idolatries and
sin, along with a concomitant confession of God's mercy, has consistently
been woven into all of our worship services.[11] As a result, confession and

8. Wright, *Evil and the Justice of God*, 99.

9. For evidence of this pattern, see Lovelace, *Dynamics of Spiritual Life* where he
focuses primarily on the signs of this pattern in the biblical narrative and the Great
Awakening in the eighteenth century.

10. The gospel of Mark announces this theme with the commencement of Jesus' public ministry: "The time is fulfilled and the kingdom of God has come near; repent, and
believe in the good news" (Mark 1:15).

11. The categories of worship presented in that paper by T. W. included: orientation
before God (humility, trust in God, praise), transformation (confession, Scripture reading, prayer, healing) and evangelization/mission (outward expression, witness, kingdom
of God, solidarity, reconciliation).

repentance are now embraced as foundational practices in the Christian life.

> *In the expression of our corporate worship, confession has grown over the last five years, it's actually something we do. There has been enough teaching about it, exposure to confession as a natural rhythm of our life together as a church that it has become safe. There is an invitation for people to confess whoever they are and where we need to grow.*

The subject matter of our confessions has also expanded from the identification of sin as the breaking of a moral command to an understanding of sin as a misshaped way of life, where our pursuits become distorted (idolatrous) or out of proportion with regard to God's vision of Shalom. Rather than confessing only our individual sins, we have taken up the practice of confessing our corporate and societal sins.

> *I think unique to this church is that we recognize cultural and social idols that we are often blind to. I have been surprised in being involved in the charismatic circle and trying to learn from them. They can recognize the idols of other cultures but there is nothing in there about our own idols in our culture which look different because they look secular rather than religious. I think our church has done a good job about seeking to identify those and part of confession is not just naming them but seeking alternative ways to live differently, to turn from them.*

A significant shift in our practice of corporate confession occurred a couple years ago when one of my colleagues preached a sermon on Daniel 8.

> *Confession is not always what we feel—but we are called to confess as an act of obedience. I am not trying to manipulate and conjure up certain emotions in you. Yet I know as a congregation we already carry the lament of the nations we come from and the nation we now live in, we are carrying in our bodies and yet it is too much to carry it within us. A confession is a release—to name our lament, our burden, name the sin, and release this to our merciful God.*

In response to this summons, one congregant reflects:

> *Two months ago, M. preached on what confession was and the work of confessing on behalf of our nation, the sins of our nation. At the*

end of that service, people were invited to come to the front or kneel or be in prayer and confessions could be spoken. Spontaneously for over twenty minutes, people just began confessing the sins of their nation, where they were from, so not just Canada. And then there was a real sense of sharing in the grief of those together, not blaming but sharing in it, and then to understand that we could pray these prayers, we could repent and be absolved. We had the idea that God had heard our prayers and forgiven us and would heal the nations. That was a tremendous time together as a body.

For the past two years, we have taken this practice of corporate confession public by participating in a "repentance walk" on Good Friday. At various stations around the neighborhood, we shared in a litany, repenting of the social sins that our community bears: unfair trade practices, ignoring homelessness, sexual exploitation, mistreatment of First Nations and busyness. As we made our way down the street, people stopped to listen to the stories of injustice and suffering and then, in some cases, join with us in repenting of these wrongs.

As the practices of confession and repentance have become more commonplace in our worship, we have witnessed both individual and corporate change within our church. *"There is hope in the confession because together in the community we are trying to figure out how we can live alternatively so it is not just a guilt or shaming but a turn from and a turning towards something else."*

In my first years as a pastor, I used to fear that newcomers might be spooked by the prospect of confession and repentance, but I have actually seen more people leave by our failure to take up this practice. When we don't initiate people in the practice of confession and repentance early on, we prevent them from entering into God's transforming power. David Janzen notes the renunciations that Jesus asks of the disciples:

> You cannot be my disciple unless . . . These renunciations include but are not limited to, personal possessions, oaths and idle talk, the right to have enemies, worry, making judgments of people God has forgiven, careers and family expectations. This list, partial as it is, seems like the heroic stuff of super-Christian. But Jesus assumed these renunciations came at the beginning of the life of discipleship.[12]

12. Janzen, "Intentional Formation," 83.

By naming these idolatries and repenting of them, we are freed to embrace the costly demands of the gospel and to live out of God's restorative power in our lives.

Towards New Life in Christ

Many of the idolatries we identified and then confronted as a congregation have infiltrated our lives subtly, persistently and pervasively pulling us into their magnetic orbit, diverting us from the pain we encounter within and around us.

> Being unable to cure death, wretchedness and ignorance, humans have decided, in order to be happy, not to think about such things. . . . I can quite see that it makes a man happy to be diverted from contemplating his private miseries by making him care about nothing else but dancing well.[13]

After our sermon series on the book of Daniel last fall, several home groups began to make space for confession and accountability around these diversions during their time together.

Entertainment

> *I just find that I am amazed that on any given Sunday millions of people are sitting in football stadiums watching the game or sitting in front of the TV and the extent that the entertainment industry can draw massive numbers of people to its events that have no meaning and significance to anybody's life and then if you call a rally or march of solidarity for indigenous or aboriginal justice, you get a handful of people.*

One of the first idolatries we confronted in our 1995 sermon series on Luke was the temptation to use our discretionary time for entertainment. So volunteering at Out of the Cold, participating in a home group, welcoming neighbors to an evening meal, or listening to a lecture on homelessness all require our willingness to forgo watching a DVD, television show or sporting event.

13. Pascal, *Pensees*, # 133 and # 137.

During this series, my family came home one evening and discovered that our television had been stolen. In its place was a note that read: "to help you during Lent." Four weeks later, we received some interesting photographs in the mail: our television in the dumpster, falling down the staircase of a Catholic cathedral, sitting atop a rock jutting out of the ocean, along with numerous other locations around the city. My family pasted these pictures onto a poster and hung it in the church hall to solicit clues as to "where it was last seen," along with a reward. Needless to say, the poster and story stimulated debate, not only about whether the pastor's television should be stolen (a point which many of the new immigrants did not find humorous), but also about the quantity of hours we as a culture spend sitting passively in front of our television screens. When our television appeared mysteriously in the sanctuary during Holy Week, I realized that I had been "cured" of excessive TV watching myself, which opened up new spaces of time for true recreation and rest, a richer taste of Sabbath. I've recommended our "thief" for other television addicts since that "miraculous" cure.

About seven years later, the residents of one of our community houses constructed a statuesque idol of old television sets on the front lawn of their house, which is situated along a busy commuter road, bringing this issue into public debate in our neighborhood. That debate widened after the Good Friday service that year, in which we lamented and repented of our obsession with both televised entertainment and technologically mediated communications. Over the years, many individuals and families have responded to this idolatry by disconnecting their cable television and curbing or eliminating their TV viewing. These actions have resulted in freedom to engage in creative ventures, develop relationships and find true rest.

At the same time, the people in our church who are vocationally committed to theater, music and the cinema have pushed the rest of us to consider the divinely created beauty of these media rather than just their mind-numbing parodies. A recent gala fundraiser, with performances by members or friends of our congregations, featured a reading from a Giller-nominated novelist, an award-winning playwright, and the gut-wrenching street poetry of an ex-addict, as well as music saturated with soul and pathos and a drama inducing delight from the audience. More than one person who had no association with our church expressed surprise that Baptists could host an evening of such powerful music, drama and literature, a comment that reveals a caricature of our denominational history, which has focused on the idolatry of entertainment without affirming or reviving the haunting and invigorating qualities present in art. That night gave us a glimpse of how the arts and media can be redeemed as pathways to God, rather than abandoned as mind-numbing diversions.[14]

Internet Surfing

> . . . what Tim shared a few weeks ago about the role that technology has taken on in our lives, taking on this kind of idolatrous mask, has been a struggle [for me]. It has repercussions for the way that our family life is, our marriage is, and the way that I interact with other people—so it is a struggle to know how to rightly hold these things to allow them to be submitted to God, without allowing them to become the controlling factor.

While the Internet has become an efficient source of disseminating and accessing information within our community, it has also become another tempting diversion, one which can keep us huddled up in our homes, "wasting" away the day and night. In the last five years, congregants have confessed their addictions to online games, YouTube, web surfing, and online pornography.

In *Habits of the High-Tech Heart,* Quentin Schultze questions the extent to which community can be formed through mediated communication and wonders whether we are losing the skills and virtues needed to develop long-term face-to-face relationships, particularly when we can just delete someone's e-mail or block them from our list of "friends" on Facebook.[15] He warns that unreflective use of communications technology will make life "increasingly empty, as entire populations become unable to discern what is valuable from what is valueless, replacing wisdom with trivial information."[16] While some have removed the Internet from

---

14. See Wright, *Simply Christian*, 3–54.
15. Schultze, *Habits of the High-Tech Heart,* 183.
16. Ibid., 69–90.

their homes, most people in our congregation are seeking ways to appreciate the benefits of this technology while resisting its addictive allure.

Workaholism

In our culture, paid work often tends towards the extremes of over or underemployment, but some folks in our community have decided to work less (by living in community or simplifying their lifestyles) in order to participate more in kingdom ventures within the church and neighborhood. Recognizing that our employment can easily become a diversion, shifting our role from "actors to bystanders,"[17] one person chose to work half-time and devote the rest of her "work" time to building up the community by volunteering with the Potter's House. After a long job search, one person with a PhD decided to carve out a teaching career through sessional work, so that he could take up part-time employment with Out of the Cold as part of his vocation. One immigrant recently turned down evening work to serve on the church council. While close to half of our congregation is blessed by the fact that their vocation and employment overlap considerably, each of us has had to resist the temptation to submerse ourselves in our work and thus fail to embrace the other life-giving aspects of the creation mandate.

But by belonging to a community that values common practices such as hospitality, service, justice seeking, prayer and contemplation, we are empowered to turn away from these vain idolatries and give our lives to living in right relationship with God, one another, our neighbors, ourselves, and the whole of creation.

Accumulating Private Wealth

When two unrelated people bought a car together, some folks in our community warned them that they were inviting trouble, for in our "car-crazed" culture,[18] they are an unquestioned necessity for many adults and remain a prominent sign of social standing. As an act of resistance to the

17. Bauman, *Society Under Siege*, 201.

18. For a critique of our "car-crazed" culture and the resulting economic, social and spiritual costs, see Kunstler, *Geography Of Nowhere*.

idolatry of personal wealth, many people in our community are choosing to share vehicles in order to free up money and time devoted to maintenance, or to give vehicle access to those who couldn't afford it.

Through our experiences of community living and hospitality, some folks have began to question the shibboleth of private house ownership, and have come to view their homes as resources for taking up these practices rather private retreats that buffer us from suffering. While acknowledging our need for regular rhythms of retreat and solitude, our homes can become objects of worship if we use them to promote our own sense of comfort, security and seclusion. 🏹

Yet figuring out how our homes can be both places of care for our immediate family and places for our neighbor in need can bring unresolved tension.

> We are trying to figure out housing issues and what is appropriate
> . . . on the one hand you want to take care of your family and provide
> for their future and things like that and on the other hand feeling
> at least something of a call to not hold onto possessions, including
> houses and things, and realizing that most people in the world have
> nothing compared to us. How do we live in this country and this
> city and this neighborhood in a way that is consistent with a call to
> identify with the poor? We are not sure how to do this.

Caring for our church building has provided a corporate tutorial in navigating through this tension.

> Our building was falling down and we had to catch up with build-
> ing it, repairing it. We've really had to work through what is the
> purpose of our building. How do we steward it? We've had to catch
> up with taking care of it. There was so much to be done, so much
> lacking. Then we were done [rebuilding], there was the feeling that
> "this is ours." We had to work through the idea. Is it OK for people
> to use this building? So if things get taken or things get broken, is it
> OK? Then they have to be repaired again. So we faced a bit of that
> idolatry with our building.

In a "private world," if a few have excess wealth and many lack access to basic housing, that is just the run of luck, but in a community where we are called to be our "brother's and sister's keeper," doing nothing feeds the idolatry of wealth. Many people from our church who once lived in Grandview Woodlands have relocated to neighborhoods with cheaper housing, either to rent or own, fragmenting our community to some extent. These departures have prompted those in our community with greater economic resources to ask how they can use their money to assist those who can't afford to live here. One person offered an interest free loan to an immigrant family, capital that they used as a down payment for purchasing a town home. The lack of affordability has stirred up innovative home ownership concepts too: two couples who desire to remain in the neighborhood long-term have jointly purchased a house together. Another family used their limited savings to buy a small house in the neighborhood and then rent out part of it in order to pursue life as part of this community.

Resisting the accumulation of private wealth will also bring us into conflict with powerful market forces. In a provocative essay, Harvey Cox examines our unquestioned allegiance to the market: "The omnipotence of The Market means that there is no conceivable limit to its inexorable ability to convert creation into commodities."[19] While considering the rent for two community houses that the church owns and leases, our council had a serious discussion about their "market value." Eventually, we agreed that providing affordable housing and supporting the vision of those houses lay at the heart of our church's vision of hospitality, and so we decided to keep the rents affordable, but ensure these houses' long-term upkeep. By resisting the market-driven assumption that the goal of life is to accumulate wealth and security, we are freed to live with a "theology of enough"[20] and to offer our resources to build up the entire community, trusting in God to grant us security amidst uncertainty and weakness.[21]

When the market impacts how our culture values human life, those who require extra "care" and money—those who are mentally ill, addicted, unemployed, or those with developmental disabilities (including unborn babies)—need us to affirm their inherent worth as humans fashioned in the Divine likeness. By welcoming such folks as worship leaders, scripture readers, interviewees and valued members of our homes, we resist the

19. Cox, "Market as God," 20.

20. Recorded in the Council minutes for October 11, 2007.

21. 2 Cor 12:9: "My grace is sufficient for you, my power is made perfect in weakness."

market's declaration of their humanity and clothe with honor those we think less "honorable."[22]

During our sermon series on work, we interviewed a fellow training to be a psychiatric nurse, and during the course of the interview (much to my surprise—and his) he shared the story of his psychotic breakdown, describing the shame and isolation he experienced. The testimony of God's grace amidst his schizophrenia struck the congregation into silence, and one newcomer, who also struggled with schizophrenia, mused later that he felt he could be understood and appreciated among us because of rather than in spite of his illness. By pursuing a kingdom vision in which the "last shall be first," we are freed to embrace the beauty and gifts of those considered less valuable.

Individualism / Autonomy

The idolatry of autonomy is evident in our reluctance to join communities and our resistance to accept demands that make us uncomfortable, even though they are often necessary to belonging.

> . . . the flight from the "messiness of real intimacy" is more akin to a herd-like stampede than to an individually conceived and un-dertaken journey of self-exploration. The secession is hardly ever lonely—the escapees are keen to join company with other escap-ees like them—and the standards of the escapee life tend to be as safe and demanding as those which have been found oppressive in the life left behind. The sole attraction of the self-chosen exile is the absence of commitments, and particularly long-term com-mitments of the kind that cramp freedom of movement in a com-munity with its "messy intimacy."[23]

These cultural assumptions regarding autonomy often conflict with our congregation's commitment to community, causing us to question whether our bonds are present only as long as we possess shared interests, or if we are, in fact, in this venture of pursuing the kingdom together. These questions have emerged whenever we have experienced conflict around theological differences, frustrations with worship, fatigue, bro-

22. 1 Cor 12:23.
23. Bauman, *Liquid Love*, 52.

ken romantic relationships within the congregation, disagreement with corporate decisions, or anger over the church's inability to get very far in implementing certain aspects of its vision.

When the Salsbury Community Society board decided not to receive funding from a major donor because of philosophical differences, a crisis arose which threatened the society's unity—as well as the unity of our church. A year or so after that decision was made, the society gathered to express honest and painful rebuke, confession, repentance, and grieving, a process that propped open the door towards healing. At the end of that weekend retreat, everyone shared communion—in unity and restored relationship—along with renewed hope for continuing on together. One person involved in this process of reconciliation comments on the pivotal role that confession played:

> I think if you don't have that place of repentance, you almost start to take sides more and you distance yourselves from others . . . If you take a posture of repentance, you are recognizing that we are in this together and we all need to be challenged. We take people from where their starting point is and we all challenge one another to take deeper places with God and operate out of a place of humility rather than of defensiveness and position-taking.

When we let go of our stubborn attachment to autonomy, we are ushered into reconciliation and belonging. Through Christ's reconciling love, a Karen man and his "enemy oppressor" from a majority ethnic group can read Scripture together, in their own languages, as brothers in Christ. These snippets of Shalom, often overshadowed by the darkness of the dissolution and disintegration, remind us of what we are missing by clinging to this idol of autonomy (and its associated vices).

Our vision of transformation will begin to change as we see that the depth of social division and how it has infected our world is deeper than we imaged. We will begin to see that pursuit of a just reconciliation is a long and costly process, requiring forgiveness, patience and hope, nurtured in practices of listening to God.[24]

Despite the idolatrous power of autonomy, which is burrowed into our collective psyche as a society, some have embraced the demands of community. One woman with a young adult daughter, who ran into

24. Rice, "Lament for Racial Divisions," 66.

repeated rejections over twenty years, testified in worship recently that she had finally found—first through Crossroads and then through the church—what she had lost hope of ever finding: a place to belong.

> Of course, this new society is not going to be very attractive for those whose hopes are set on success in the present order. But it will fill with longing those for whom this present world is not working, those left behind by globalization, those stuck in the burned out places in the empire, those who have tasted success in the world and found it empty of meaning.[25]

Family

> *I think that one of our idolatries . . . is family and our perception of what a family should be and I think it is associated with this whole idea of isolation to community as well.*

Rodney Clapp argues that the family, specifically the nuclear family, has morphed into a haven of refuge from the hardships of life, a justification for non-involvement in civic life or public participation.[26] As such, "family" has become an acceptable reason for not participating in these trajectories. Our own captivity to our children's sporting involvements, which of course bring many benefits, can occupy five or six evenings a week. One person identifies this overloaded focus on the family as a common phenomena: "*A lot of people are simply thinking of themselves, my children, my home, and that is it.*"

Though a surprise to many folks within and beyond the church, Jesus places loyalty to himself and his kingdom above family loyalties when (in a strong aphorism) he warns his followers that anyone who "does not hate father and mother, wife and children, brothers and sisters, and even life itself, cannot be my disciple."[27] On the other hand, Jesus upheld the marriage covenant and valued children over and above his disciples' diminution of them.[28]

25. Janzen, "Intentional Formation," 88.
26. Clapp, *Families at the Crossroads*, 15.
27. Luke 14:26.
28. Cf. Matt 19:3–9; Mark 10:13–16.

The challenge before our congregation has been to resist both the idolatry of family and the idolatry of autonomy, which fractures families and leads to parental neglect. Naming and confessing both these idolatries has freed us to offer more support to families, particularly as the number of families with young children has multiplied in our church and parents have begun requesting resources for marriage and parenting. One person who has organized parenting classes in our church concurs:

> I think one of the starting points is a responsive community. Seeing people isolated or hearing from people that they feel lonely, [that] they don't have the resources and they are not sure how to make the next steps, trying to respond with resources like education and support and advocacy in terms of problem-solving.

Our children's ministry coordinator has begun offering resources to parents so that they can develop traditions of prayer, Scripture reading, and discussion at home, and we have developed a marriage support group, although more are needed. One sign of hope is that most of the marriages have found enough support to continue in covenant: of the thirty-five marriages I have officiated at GCBC, thirty-one are still working at the art of love.

Seeking to navigate the rough waters between the idolatries of autonomy and family, we have sought the flourishing of nuclear families *within* a community of people pursuing the reign of God. While my son and I were chatting about his school over breakfast a few years ago, he told me that he had noticed a difference between the adult men he knew (and hung out with) from our church and his male teachers. "*My teachers talk a good talk, but they don't walk the walk like the guys at church do.*" During adolescence, when children establish their own identity apart from parents, I have been grateful to be surrounded by people who model the way of Christ and take an interest in our children. Belonging to a community of care has freed our family from isolation and enfolded our children in a wider womb of meaning and love.

One person whose family has shared their home with students and then homeless neighbors affirms the importance of modeling for her own children that their family is not an end in itself:

> *I think from living on our own . . . we were isolated in our own*
> *insular family. I can remember having discussions about that, that*
> *our family isn't everything. We have to be more outward focused or*
> *your family becomes more self-centered; you are modeling a self-*
> *centered isolationism.*

These Trajectories as Idols

One irony of taking up these practices is that they themselves can become
idols if they are not continually pursued within the context of the kingdom of God. "*Even our own community can sometimes be idolatry itself*
because many churches are just happy with their own fuzzy community."

But a cozy community sought for its own sake does not lead us deeper into transformation within ourselves and our neighborhood, because
community itself cannot replace our deeper need for life centered in the
divine Trinity. Ringma offers this discerning route for those who seek to
live as part of a community:

> To hold what is good and to let go what is unhelpful or undesir-
> able requires more than mere discernment. It requires an aban-
> donment to the God who both holds us fast and shelters and
> nurtures us and who empowers and releases us.[29]

Over a decade ago, when two full-time professors at a local theological graduate school joined our congregation, they drew many students to
the incarnational, neighborhood-focused, kingdom vision of our church.
As we encouraged these students to live in the neighborhood and to initiate friendships with non-students, some folks felt alienated by the flood
of academically oriented young adults who were "taking over our church"
or "just coming because it was cool." "Community is put in jeopardy once
people start gushing over how great their community is and tell people
who oppose it to shut up."[30] So rather than focusing on how relevant or

---

29. Ringma, *Seek the Silences*, 14.

30. Bauman, *Community*, 10. Chris Rice offers a pertinent warning for any Christian
community that is finding creative paths to implementing a kingdom vision: "It has always been a great temptation for especially fervent Christians to think that they are so
superior to other Christians of lesser commitment that they do not need to associate
with them. But to succumb to this temptation is to fall prey to the greatest sin of all, the
sin of pride—and to the worst form of pride, which is spiritual pride. When this great

leading edge our community is perceived to be, we have invited these new students to embrace the practices that have shaped us: hospitality to the stranger, mutual understanding across cultural differences, and seeking beauty and justice for the least within our neighborhood.

Like community, cultural diversity can also be an idol.

> *Is this just a different tribe? Or is it a transformed tribe? Because I think the danger is that we become something that then we defend and we become isolated in our own tribalism. . . . integrated multi-cultural living on its own might just be a different kind of tribalism.*

A few years ago, we invited two immigrants onto our church council, a practice we had followed for most of my tenure at the church, in order to reflect our diverse ethnic composition as a community. However, these particular council members became less vocal at our meetings and increasingly passive about taking up responsibilities through their year of service, until one quit altogether. By placing them on council without providing mentors to guide them in their function as council members, we allowed our desire for "the look of diversity" to replace an actual commitment to the practice of embracing diversity.

Eight years ago, a pastor from a neighboring church took us to task when he perceived that we were content to provide a meal and shelter as our only response to the issues of homelessness, perpetuating government inaction.

> *I suppose even charity itself can be an idolatry . . . . somehow we think that by our crumbs from the table, that somehow things will get fixed out there. There is a big problem of poverty and homeless-ness we are seeing out there. If we relinquish our duty to actually influence the society, then we are just hoping that crumbs will fix it. Charities are the wheel of making you feel good.*

Without pursuing a transformed order that reflects God's justice, our Out of the Cold meal might let the rest of society—government, business, neighbors—abdicate their responsibility to care for the least.

---

evil enters our lives, as it does in every Christian's life as some point, we lose any sense of needing others. We lose any capacity to learn from others, any chance of having our faults corrected by others and any hope of serving them since everyone quickly senses spiritual pride and is repulsed by it" ("Lament for Racial Divisions," 73).

One of the activists in our church has recently distanced herself from our worshipping life, criticizing us for not doing enough or being quick enough in our pursuit of social justice. While she may well be right, it is hard to see how her decision to leave will help the church move further in its pursuit of justice.

> . . . *in advocacy, I think the idolatry of the "we're right they're wrong" judgment and anger. They are actually harmful. Judgment and anger against the systems, which is not bad, can warp you to turn into a bitterness that does not help.*

Another member names this danger in seeking justice:

> *Justice movements can be fuelled by hatred and anger and I think deeper life in God frees us for the same justice movement to be fuelled from a place of creativity and love. To me they are two completely different things and so that is where again we have made this comment that this fourth [trajectory] needs to inform these ones, because I think if we are moving here we are moving into a different type of justice seeking that actually is liberating everybody in the process rather than just creating a new dichotomy that has perpetuated itself all through history.*

In pursuing these trajectories, we can easily forget the patience that others have demonstrated with us and allow pride in our progression, or in our particular practice, to trump all other pursuits of the kingdom.

One question that is helpful in assessing whether or not these trajectories are slipping into idolatry is to examine our reasons for pursuing them: are we pursuing goods external to this practice or intrinsic to it?[31] For example, the pursuit of justice for the least may bring the opportunity to yank the rich and arrogant down from their lofty ground or to separate one's self from an uninvolved, pietistic church. But both of these goals exist independently from the pursuit, so it would be external—and idolatrous. But when seeking justice for the least is pursued as an expression of the kingdom of God, with the goal of participating in the reign of God and the divine life, then one is pursuing internal goods, goods that are intrinsic to this trajectory.

---

31. Wilson discusses the difference between external and internal goods, based on the ideas of Alasdair MacIntyre's writing, in *Living Faithfully in a Fragmented World*, 35–38.

Many of the idols discussed in this chapter find their root in the idolatry of self, or more specifically, the false self: ⅄

> I think that the essential idolatry for me is myself . . . if you ever end up in radical hospitality with your false self still intact, it is just going to be a recipe for disaster because you won't be able to create the relational space that's needed for others who presumably who will be in there with you. You need some people operating out of a place of God-self or true self in these environments. [Then] others who may still be very defensive or protective people can come in and be transformed themselves.

The fact that these trajectories can become idols has led us to the expanded awareness that persisting in the venture that Jesus called the kingdom of God is no simple excursion: if we are to keep moving towards this vision, we need to grow deeper into the new life in Christ and the divine life of the Trinity, the next and final step in this trajectory.

> Radical hospitality, integrated multicultural living, and the seeking justice for the least—those on their own might just be a different kind of tribalism. But this—deeper life in God—is what in the end moves everything into a new way. ✗

When awareness for our need for God deepens, it becomes the necessary impetus that prompts us to discover the resources within the Christian tradition for moving ever deeper into the divine life of the Trinity.

EIGHT

Navigating into the River of Life

God's inner nature and life should be opened up to us, should become familiar to us, and we should experience with our very being, and hence also with our minds and senses, what it means to say that God is love.[1]

As we have persevered in the practices of radical hospitality, integrated multicultural living and seeking justice for the least over the past twenty years, we have come to a greater awareness that we must find deeper renewal in our life with God if we are going to be sustained on this long and arduous journey.

> *I think our church is very good at moving outward in a broad way, but [we need to] . . . come to the place of saying there is a deeper participation in the life of God.*

Unless we are "rooted and built up in Christ," we will have no hope in continuing along these demanding kingdom trajectories.[2]

> *I basically came to an end of what I felt like we could do . . . on my own strength, even all of us together . . . [Though] a lot of what we have here is good . . . it's so fragile and so pieced together and . . . we don't know what we are doing most of the time . . . [If] there is no sense that God is . . . moving in a way that is greater and powerful and has a vision that we are not even aware of, it is kind of futile and meaningless. So that need opened me up to more renewal.*

1. Balthasar, *Prayer*, 179.
2. Col 2:6–7.

The testimony of this woman who has been a part of GCBC for almost a decade bears witness to this need to participate in the divine life of the Trinity.

> I was in the midst of desert time with grieving with my dad and the fire in our house and I felt like that was kind of the end, my faith was disappearing, I felt it slipping through my fingers, but [in] conversations with M., she said, "Have you ever noticed that Jesus went into the desert led by the Spirit but went out empowered by the Spirit?" [and that] gave me hope, that maybe this desert is not a backsliding, or that my faith is disappearing as much as it is something I am being brought through. And maybe there has been a stripping or letting go of something as well as hope that the desert will end at some point, a longing to be empowered by the Spirit.

Thankfully, that life of prayer has been cultivated among us: as the hard ground of our lives has been tilled by the exposures of our idolatries and our need to turn to God, new practices of prayer have sprouted, moving us further into divine communion.

> I think we are just praying more. We are beginning to understand more that prayer and this work of relating to God and letting God relate to us and teach us in prayer is just becoming part of the fabric of our church. I see it happening more in home groups, in the prayer service at the end of each year that the church has, in the prayer week that we have at the beginning of each New Year. I see it in the groups of people that get together for prayer spontaneously . . . I see it at Stillpointe [where] more and more people are coming on their own for prayer and meditation, participating in the rhythms of prayer that happen there during the week, and more and more groups are beginning not only to talk about prayer in their initiatives—like Reed, or Crossroads, or Salsbury—but they are beginning to pray.

As our need for an open and receptive life centred in God grew, we began dipping our toes into the practices of prayer and Scripture reading/reflection that we have inherited from the ancient church. While our primary discourse around prayer for the first decade focused around intercession and thanksgiving, our practice of prayer has widened—in our worship, small groups, personal lives, and in the very streets of our neighborhood[3]—through exposure to the church's treasures of prayer and an expanding theology of prayer. Lectio Divina, contemplative prayer, listening prayer, prophetic prayer, and practicing the presence of God have all been taken up as practices to orient us towards the One who sustains us and for whom our hearts long. Gradually, God has raised up among us mentors who are apprenticing others in the practices of healing prayer, listening prayer and contemplative prayer. Our theology of prayer has shifted from understanding prayer as an instrument for moving God to action towards dwelling in God, who moves us towards a new identity and new action.[4] Learning to dwell in God or to "practice the presence of God" has become a source of strength for a growing number of people in our community.

Renewal has also come through a burgeoning interest in spiritual direction and spiritual retreats. M., who started Stillpointe, a place for prayer and retreat in the city, comments on the increased desire for spiritual direction.

> *I think if you want to live following Christ in this world, you are going to have questions, and you are going to . . . need to know how then to live, in a way that is different than how you lived before, in a way that is about learning to listen to God, and learning to hear God. Like Jesus said, "My sheep know my voice, they know my command, and they follow me." That is a picture of an intimate knowing and people want to know God and be known. So spiritual direction is a listening ear and a space for people to begin to know God.*

My colleague, T., nurtured this practice of God's presence through her teaching on contemplation, both through sermons and her passionate modeling of contemplation as she invited us to observe the movements of God in our everyday lives.

One of the ongoing challenges we face is discerning how justice and spirituality fit together. Within Crossroads, some of the staff and volunteers have discerned this disjunction and are developing a "working theol-

---

3. Prayer walks are the preferred mode of prayer for some people in our community.

4. This shift is evident especially in the litanies that have been composed for our worship by members of the congregation. For each season of the year, new litanies have been composed that we have then utilized for that period of time.

ogy" paper to address this fissure.[5] Many others within our community are longing to live into a greater integration of these practices.

> At heart, the contemplative is one who sees clearly, sees with the eyes of God, the clear light which shines in the emptiness of the human spirit. It is clear vision which enables the truly spiritual person to see beneath the surface of events, to see through the illusion and the phoney claims of human systems, to see beyond the immediate and the transient to the reality. Consequently, the contemplative is more of a threat to injustice than the social activist who merely sees the piecemeal need. For contemplative vision is revolutionary vision and it is the achievement of this vision which is the fruit of true spiritual direction.[6]

Through contemplation, we realize that the search for God is a search for One who is already seeking us. "Human desire describes that longing, that thirst, for God which God's grace has instilled in human hearts—and which remains unfulfilled except through friendship with God."[7] God's love pulls us towards these trajectories, which lead us to confront our idolatries, exposing our deeper need for God. This spiraling pattern leads us ever deeper into new life with Christ. *It is when I am secure in the love of God that I am willing to face my idolatry and move deeper into the new life in Christ.*

In our annual week of prayer at the New Year, a newcomer signed up to pray for an hour during our 24-hour prayer clock. Though he had never prayed before, he used our prayer guide, and as he shared during his baptism six months later, "*God became real to me in that hour.*"

We do not pray easily in our culture, even when we are aware of our need for God. As we have journeyed along the road towards divine communion, we have encountered numerous barriers that have led us off the trail. One such barrier is our distorted image of God, a perception that:

> *God is distant, that God does not care, that God loves everyone else but me, that God cannot heal or will not, that God should heal now and on my terms and with my expectations . . . There is a distortion of who we are before God.*

---

5. See the Crossroads minutes of November 14th, 2007.

6. Leech, *Soul Friend*, 191.

7. Jones, "Thirst for God or Consumer Spirituality," 3–28.

This distorted image of God is often connected to wounds from close relationships. If we are to overcome this barrier between ourselves and God, as well as other people, we will need God's healing, and so a ministry of inner healing has slowly taken root in our congregations. Through extended times of prayer, two people pray with and for the person seeking healing, inviting her through a series of prayers, including confession and repentance. Our experience with healing prayer has confirmed that confession and repentance are God's gifts, given to liberate us from bondage into the land of freedom, where we recover our God-imaging vocation and uncover the resources of love found in the divine Trinity.[8]

As we have moved through confession and repentance in healing prayer, it has been important to help those seeking healing to confess and repent for those sins that were committed against themselves as well as sins committed in reaction to those wrongs. This has been particularly critical when praying for someone who has been wronged, abused or exploited. By naming the wrongs done to oneself in the presence of God, forgiving the oppressor and confessing one's own chains to resentment or bitterness, God graciously leads us from the darkness of captivity to the healing light of freedom.

> When you live in such close proximity to people, you rub against each other and you recognize your own woundedness and your own baggage and also you get hurt the more you are connected with people. So it has been important for me over time in different ways to have avenues for confession and repentance and inner healing prayer . . . to move through those things.

Another barrier we have encountered in our journey towards deeper life in God is the secularism of our age, a functional atheism that infects our desire to live in the presence of God.[9]

8. The need for inner healing arises when we discover blocks or barriers to loving God and others freely. The need for inner healing, which is present for nearly all of us at some junctures in our lives, should be distinguished from the therapeutic desire to "feel good" all the time, which is quite a different way of evaluating our wholeness or wellness. See Payne, *Healing Presence*, 170–71 and Ringma, *Seek the Silences*, 26–27.

9. See Taylor's brilliant analysis of how secularism has developed in *A Secular Age*. Two key factors he identifies in this move are the drive to organization, leading to arrangements that disallow God's involvement, and the reality that jettisoning flawed ways of conceptualizing God's involvement in the world has led to jettisoning the idea of God's involvement entirely.

> For most of us then, God is more of a moral and intellectual prin-
> ciple than a person and our commitment to this principle runs
> the gamut from fiery passion, wherein persons are willing to die
> for a cause, to a vague nostalgia, wherein God and religion are
> given the same type of status and importance as is given the royal
> family in England, namely, they are the symbolic anchor for a cer-
> tain way of life but they are hardly important in its day-to-day
> functioning. It is not that this is bad, it is just that one does not
> see much evidence that anyone is actually all that interested in
> God. We are interested in virtue, justice, a proper way of life and
> perhaps even in building communities for worship, support and
> justice, but, in the end, too much evidence suggests that moral
> philosophies, human instinct and a not so disguised self interest
> are more important in motivating these activities than are a love
> and a gratitude that stem from a personal relationship to a living
> God. Hence, God is not only often absent in our marketplaces,
> he is also frequently absent from our religious activities as well.[10]

Related to the barrier of functional atheism is our tendency to become so immersed in our projects and their impact for change that we
forget God. God simply becomes an instrument to achieve our goals, a
distant object whom we seek to control for our ends. While we have regularly critiqued the consumerist spirituality that "treats God as our personal trainer,"[11] we can make the same error in pursuing these practices
if we are not continually assessing our attachment to our own projects
within the greater context of our primary attachment to God.

TOWARDS INTERIORIZED MONASTICISM

In *The Dark Night of the Soul*, St. John of the Cross argues that when we
come to the end of ourselves and our displaced devotion to attachments
other than God, we are invited into divine friendship.

> What do you think serving God involves other than avoiding evil,
> keeping his commandments, and being occupied with the things

---

10. Rolheiser, *Shattered Lantern*, 16.

11. I used this metaphor in a sermon a year ago and it elicited some resistance in
our own home group, partly because it touched a nerve. See also Jones's perceptive essay
listed above.

of God as best we can? When this is had, what need is there of other apprehensions or other lights and satisfactions from this source or that? In these there is hardly ever a lack of stumbling blocks and dangers for the soul, which by its understanding and appetites is deceived and charmed; and its own faculties cause it to err. And thus God does one a great favour when he darkens the faculties and impoverishes the soul in such a way that one cannot err with these.[12]

If we are to find our primary attachment within God, the monastic tradition has much to offer us. The vows of poverty, chastity and obedience, as Paul Evdokimov writes, "constitute a great charter of human liberty. Poverty frees us from the ascendancy of the material . . . Chastity frees us from the ascendancy of the carnal . . . Obedience frees us from the idolatry of the ego."[13] While Evdokimov does not forecast a swelling of the monasteries, he does envision an "interiorized monasticism" among followers of Christ, an adoption of the monastic vows within everyday life, if the church is to be faithful to God in a postmodern world. "Prayer, fasting, the reading of Scripture and ascetic disciplines are imposed on all by the same prescription."[14] Seeking to live from this center of life in the Trinity.

While a growing number of people in our community have been flirting with vows of poverty (or frugality or simplicity), chastity and obedience, perhaps it is time for at least some to form a lay order and commit themselves to such vows openly, initiating others into this Trinitarian way of life and maturing our community. At the least, if we hope to continue as a people committed to embracing the practices of radical hospitality, integrated multicultural life and seeking justice for the least, we will need to nurture the seeds of an interiorized monasticism, that we may together journey towards deeper life in God.

12. St. John of the Cross, *Complete Works*, 755.

13. Evdokimov, *Ages of the Spiritual Life*, 139. I understand chastity along the lines that Ronald Rolheiser defines it. "Chastity is not the same thing as celibacy. To be chaste does not mean that one does not have sex . . . . To be chaste is to experience people, things, places, entertainment, the phases of our lives and sex in a way that does not violate them or ourselves. To be chaste is to experience things reverently." Rolheiser, *Holy Longing*, 201–2.

14. Evdokimov, *Ages of the Spiritual Life*, 137. For a popular book that highlights the appeal of monasticism today, see Norris, *Cloister Walk*.

> *[Life] does force people to have to deepen their life with God, or they just leave. It is not just our church, so many people and many friends of mine don't go to church anymore. People who have been long-time church-goers and have been leaders in churches totally leave church.*

If this long ride into the reign of God is to continue, fused with joy and hope, only love, the love overflowing from the Father, the Son, and the Spirit, can lead us onward. "Service needs to be shaped more by the magic of love than by the psychology of our compulsions. And in the long run, it is only love that will fuel us for the long journey of faithful service."[15] The question before us now is whether or not we will make room to receive this divine love.

Reshaping Desire

> Congregations ought to be settings for catechesis in which desires are shaped by faithful instruction and inquiry, prayer and worship, and other corporate practices that are constitutive of the church's life.[16]

Not only do we need good theology and good practices to become a gospel-shaped community, we also need to identify the gaps between our beliefs and practices. Speaking of Jonah's failure in his mission to the Ninevites, Amy Plantinga Pauw writes:

> The problem is not that Jonah fails to believe the right things; he fails to desire the right things. As the Augustinian tradition insists, the link between belief and practice is forged by human desire and attitude. Both our cognitive and practical efforts arise out of our loves. Right beliefs are by themselves insufficient in shaping good practice.[17]

As we seek to reshape and renew our desires for God, for our neighbor and for the new sort of world Jesus envisions, our captivity to the

---

15. Ringma, *Seek the Silences*, 25. For a fruitful exploration of the divine love within the Trinity and its implications for our relationship to God and one another, see Grenz, *Social God*, 304–36.

16. Jones, "Beliefs, Desires, Practices," in Volf and Bass, *Practicing Theology*, 202.

17. Ibid., 45.

cultural assumptions of the good life will be exposed, giving us courage to pursue the alternative vision for life found in Scripture. As we foster the habit of moving towards this kingdom vision, we will alter the way we order our lives, and our desires will be liberated from the cultural forces that have captured and misdirected them.[18] Bauman suggests that our consumer addiction is no longer fuelled by mere desire, but by wish fulfillment.[19]

Bernard of Clairvaux also sought to redirect desire, through confession and repentance, so that God could embolden our passion for good:

> Thus, anger, when controlled, becomes the vehicle of good zeal; pride brought low can be pressed into service in defence of justice. . . . If a strong sexuality is brought under control and disciplined by the practices of works of mercy, the very quarter whence people are exposed to the darts of wickedness becomes itself an incitement to solicitude for others.[20]

As Rolheiser has argued, spirituality can be defined as what we direct our desires toward:

> Spirituality is about what we do with the fire inside of us, about how we channel our *eros*. And how we do channel it, the disciplines and habits we choose to live by, will either lead to a greater integration or disintegration within our bodies, minds and souls and to a greater integration or disintegration in the way we are related to God, others and the cosmic world.[21]

Within our congregation, these practices have begun to reshape and redirect our desires away from consumption and wish fulfillment towards God and the kingdom of God. I now hear much less talk about finding a dream home and much more talk about how we can share our homes with those who need one. As we form communities that bear witness to a different way of ordering human life in a consumer culture, "Christianity is reclaimed as a fully material or embodied reality (The Word became

---

18. Bell argues that our desire has been captured by the present madness of "savage capitalism," an unfettered capitalism that slowly and surely is being shorn from the welfare state or public investment (*Liberation Theology after the End of History*, 10–12).

19. Bauman, *Society Under Siege*, 185.

20. LeClerq, *Monks and Love*, 16.

21. Rolheiser, *Holy Longing*, 11.

flesh), whose practices—such as baptism, catechesis, Eucharist, discipline, prayer, and discipleship—do not merely mediate 'ideas' and 'values' but rather transform the material circumstances of Christian (and more generally, human) existence."[22]

22. Bell, *Liberation Theology after the End of History*, 87.

NINE

Plunging into the Reign of God

With Vancouver's extensive coastline along the Pacific, our church usually gathers for baptisms at the ocean rather than using our baptistery. As we assemble on the oceanfront after a shared picnic meal, we listen to the testimonies of those being baptized and then head out to the water.

But several years ago, as we gathered at the beach after church, we discovered that, having neglected to check the tide charts, we had arranged to have baptisms during one of the lowest tides of the year. As a result, our flock had to journey over the sandy ocean floor for nearly a quarter mile before we reached water that was deep enough to immerse the novitiates. As our crowd of seventy people made that long trek towards the baptismal waters, several made comparisons to the wilderness wanderings of the Hebrew people. After persevering together all the way to the water's edge and then back, we noticed that our footprints had formed a collective witness to our path in the sand. This image continues to serve as a parable of our church's journey over the past two decades, as we have been transformed from a dying urban church into a community that bears witness to the kingdom and reign of God.

Like the children of Israel, we have travelled through the wilderness towards a land filled with milk and honey—as well as new idolatries and rebellions. But as we have embraced the practices of hospitality, integrated multicultural living, seeking justice for the least and participating in the new life in Christ, our neighborhood has witnessed the slow, transforming power of the gospel within us. This has given us credibility to tell our neighbors the story of a man who loved people, gathered them into community, welcomed them back to God and to one another, laid down his life for them, and rose from the dead to new life. And it has also given us credibility to tell the story of our community, a people flawed and broken, who are discovering new life together, united by the Spirit, as we seek to welcome the neighborhood back to God and to welcome our neighbors into God's new creation.

The tributary we have traveled, a tributary leading to the great river called the reign of God, is wide, slow moving, with countless eddies and rapids, but there is a current of divine goodness that continues to pull us forward. We trust that this current will carry us, along with the many other paddlers who have travelled their own tributaries, towards the mouth of this river of life, the place in which God's reign will be experienced in all its fullness.[1] Our wild hope is that the Spirit will continue to accompany us and all communities of the kingdom as we continue this long paddle into the great River of God, our only true home.

1. Rev 22:1–3.

APPENDIX

Fellow Paddlers

VOICES OF PREPARATION

> When the social order no longer upholds the church's value in
> society, reconsidering what the church is all about provides an
> occasion to retrieve the church's mission as part of the mission of
> God and to recover a renewed vision of the gospel.[1]

> Indeed, in a world which is often at odds with the vision of the
> kingdom, the church must consciously resist the powerful idols
> of our time if it is to avoid being marginalized by the forces of our
> society which view religion as a private experience with little or
> no public value.[2]

In my own preparation for leadership in our urban church, four voices
were significant in awakening this transforming vision of the gospel and
the church's engagement with the world: N. T. Wright,[3] Lesslie Newbigin,
Ray Bakke and John Perkins. Wright argues that the New Testament books
illuminate Jesus' life, death and resurrection as the climactic moment in
God's mission to overcome evil and idolatry and lead creation towards

1. So argues Bosch, *Transforming Mission*, 4.

2. Newbigin, *Foolishness to the Greeks*, 10–24.

3. Of Wright's many works, the three major volumes in his series on the origins of
Christian faith offer the fullest treatment of his work. See Wright, *New Testament and
the People of God*, *Jesus and the Victory of God*, and *Resurrection of the Son of God*. I also
had the privilege of taking three courses from him: one on the synoptic gospels in the
summer of 1988, Romans in 1992 and Philippians in 1995.

completion, thereby reconciling humanity and creation back to God. As Jesus was to Israel, so the church is to the world.[4] Following this herme-neutic, just as Jesus welcomed the lost, held rulers to account, challenged how society values people, and called people to repent and turn back to God, so also the church participates in God's mission in the particular context where it is located. The main difference between the church's mission and Jesus is that we proclaim him as the king, the one who has defeated the powers of evil and is now reconciling all things to himself. We bear witness in our life together and in our mission in the world to the ongoing reconciling and restoring work of God through Christ by the Spirit.

Wright's vision of Jesus and metanarrative of scripture compels and challenges the church to participate in the transforming power of the Spirit by being fully involved in its surrounding culture and neighbor-hood. While I didn't know how that vision could be worked out in East Vancouver, I did come to Grandview Calvary Baptist Church with a de-sire to discover how our congregation could address the world's injustice, our desire for beauty and our longing for relationship with God and each other.[5]

By pointing to some of the distinct differences between gospel liv-ing and our (post)-modernist culture, Lesslie Newbigin challenges local congregations to wonder and dream about how to overcome the divisions and idolatries of Western culture.[6]

Ray Bakke, an urban theologian and practitioner, helped me to make that vision more culturally relevant and contextual in my own urban set-ting of East Vancouver. His book, *The Urban Christian,* was my primary guide in exegeting my neighborhood and in networking with other people concerned for the welfare of our part of the city.

Around the same time, I encountered John Perkins and his three R's of Christian community development: relocation, reconciliation and redistribution.[7] His commitment to relocation influenced Mary (my wife)

---

4. This reference is found in my class notes from the summer of 1988.

5. See Wright, *Simply Christian.*

6. See Newbigin, *Gospel in a Pluralist Society,* 3–13.

7. See Perkins, *With Justice For All.*

and myself to live in the neighborhood and to invite some others who had moved away to consider moving back.

CONVERSATION PARTNERS ALONG THE WAY

After Alasdair MacIntyre's seminal work on the nature of ethics[8] and the rise of narrative theology, theologians have named and reflected upon the practices that arise out of the biblical narrative that sustain and flesh out the Christian vision.[9] Bass and Dykstra define Christian practices as: "things Christian people do together over time to address fundamental human needs in response to and in the light of Gods active presence for the life of the world."[10]

Miroslav Volf [11] argues that the taking up of practices leads people into God's transformational mission by helping them to break free from the unhealthy dualisms that keep us in captivity to the distorting powers in our culture. Evangelically rooted churches can so easily slip into the formation of biblically literate people without seeking the formation of disciples of Christ.

By taking up the practices of community, hospitality, justice and confession, our congregation, church and neighborhood have been transformed as we have sought ways to resist the powerful forces of our culture, including advertising, consumerism, the reach of the market into almost every aspect of our lies, fragmented living and geographical mobility in the climb to the "better life."

Jonathan Wilson's book *Living Faithfully in a Fragmented World* calls for the development of a new monasticism to stimulate the church to recapture its participation in the mission of God in our day.[12] These

---

8. See MacIntyre, *After Virtue.*

9. See Bass and Volf, *Practicing Theology* and Christine Pohl, *Making Room.*

10. Dykstra and Bass, "A Theological Understanding of Christian Practices," 18.

11. Volf, "Introduction," 6.

12. At the end of his book (68–69), Wilson quotes Alasdair McIntyre from *After Virtue:* "If my account of our moral condition is correct, we ought also to conclude that for some time now, we too have reached that turning point. What matters at this state is the construction of local forms of community within which civility and the intellectual and moral life can be sustained through the new dark ages, which are already upon us. And if the tradition of the virtues was able to survive the horrors of the last dark ages,

new monastic movements bear a marked resemblance to GCBC and the particular trajectories that we have explored throughout this book.

New Monasticism traces its roots back to a letter written by Dieterich Bonhoeffer in January of 1935:

> The restoration of the church will surely come from a new kind of monasticism, which will have nothing in common with the old but a life of uncompromising adherence to the Sermon on the Mount in imitation of Christ. I believe the time has come to rally people together for this.[13]

Jonathan Wilson-Hartgrove, a spokesperson for this movement, writes that the thrust of these new communities may well be "to ask in the face of our world's greatest problems what it might look like for the people of God to live together according to Jesus' Sermon on the Mount."[14] In a personal conversation, Wilson-Hartgrove told me that when he talked to Christians across America, both liberals and conservatives, nearly all of them told him how hard they thought it would be to really do the things that Jesus talked about, especially those he taught in the Sermon on the Mount. This desire to follow Jesus more concretely has motivated our own community to live a more integrated and transformed way of life.

In the seminal book from New Monastic communities, *School(s) of Conversion*, the authors identify twelve marks of New Monasticism.[15]

---

we are not entirely without grounds for hope. This time, however, the barbarians are not waiting beyond the frontiers; they have already been among us for quite some time. And it is our lack of consciousness of this that constitutes part of our predicament. We are waiting not for Godot, but for another—doubtless very different—St. Benedict" (263).

13. Cited in Wilson-Hartgrove, "Beatitudes in the Desert," 60.

14. Wilson-Hartgrove, "Beatitudes in the Desert," 61.

15. Rutba House, *Schoools of Conversion.* The twelve marks are:

1) Relocation to the abandoned places of the Empire (which was an intentional choice we made ourselves eighteen years ago).

2) Sharing economic resources with fellow community members and the needy among us (which has included sharing homes, tables, cars, lawnmowers and cash).

3) Hospitality to the stranger (which has become basic to our discipleship). This welcome includes the development of a weekly meal and shelter for the homeless—Out of the Cold/Crossroads; community houses—Salsbury community society; welcome to children—Urban Promise day camps and tutoring; and single mothers—The Open Door.

When I first read this book, I had a moment of discovery when I realized, like a child finding his first fiddler crab hiding under a rock on an ocean beach, that all twelve of these marks have been pursued by some within our church. Finding other communities of Christians around North America who were pursuing (may) of these same practices confirmed that the Spirit was guiding us, and we were encouraged to realize that we had paddled into a much broader tributary than we had first imagined.

Walter Bruggemann illustrates how choosing solidarity with the poor and suffering can awaken satiated folks from their numbness and apathy, that they might turn to God and thereby discover resurrection hope.[16] By sharing in solidarity with the suffering, our community has been awakened from the numbing effects of culture and alerted to new possibilities in the power of God.

4) Lament for racial divisions within the church and our communities combined with the active pursuit of a just reconciliation (which was already present when I arrived and which we have become more intentional about since).

5) Humble submission to Christ's body, the church (which we have continued to pursue as part of a denomination).

6) Intentional formation in the way of Christ and the rule of the community along the lines of the old novitiate (which included an identification and focus upon six practices three years ago).

7) Nurturing common life among members of intentional community (which began as a feature of our family life over sixteen years ago).

8) Support for celibate singles alongside monogamous married couples and their children (which has been a model in most of our community homes).

9) Geographical proximity to community members who share a common rule of life (which has been important in our neighborhood).

10) Care for the plot of God's earth given to us along with support of our local economies (which a number of people have taken up as their vocation).

11) Peacemaking in the midst of violence and conflict resolution within communities along the lines of Matthew 18 (which has been a model for reconciliation within our church and in our neighborhood).

12) Commitment to a disciplined contemplative life (which has grown with the designation of an apartment dedicated to different forms of prayer).

One of the major differences between these new monastic groups and our church is that, from what I can surmise, most of these communities are on the fringe of the church while these marks are at the core of who we are and where we are headed as a church.

16. See Bruggemann, *Prophetic Imagination*.

Zygmunt Bauman, a sociologist, gives a penetrating analysis of globalization and how culture shapes desire,[17] of the tension between our desire for community and autonomy,[18] of the tenuous nature of human bonds,[19] and of the way in which bureaucracy shapes society,[20] alerting our community to the powerful idolatries and forces that have (mis) shaped our society, such as individualism, autonomy, the market and wish fulfillment as a way of life.

Charles Taylor, one of the world's pre-eminent social philosophers, has shaped my historical understanding of our perception of ourselves as humans, and in particular our move towards individualism and secularism.[21]

Our church's shift from understanding to action has been influenced by liberation theology and our congregation's experience in Latin America. I had the privilege of being in Latin America three times, once during the twenty-fifth anniversary of the death of Archbishop Oscar Romero, whose pastoral model in the face of injustice continues to inspire and instruct my own work.[22] The focus on praxis in the work of liberation theologians has given us resources for working in our neighborhood and also challenged our congregation to move further towards political and social responses to injustice.[23]

Discovering these fellow paddlers along the way has fueled our theological imaginations and encouraged us to keep paddling through the sometimes turbulent waters of our particular tributary as we follow the Kingdom Way into the Great River that is the Reign of God.

---

17. Bauman, *Society Under Siege.*

18. Bauman, *Community.*

19. Bauman, *Liquid Love.*

20. Bauman, *Modernity and the Holocaust.*

21. Taylor, *Sources of the Self; Secular Age.*

22. Romero, *Violence of Love.*

23. Some of the primary sources here have been Gutierrez, *Theology of Liberation;* Sobrino, *Witnesses to the Kingdom;* and Bell, *Liberation Theology after the End of History.*

BIBLIOGRAPHY

Alexander, Bruce K. *The Roots of Addiction in Free Market Society*. Vancouver: Canadian Centre for Policy Alternatives, 2001.

Allen, Diogenes. *Christian Belief in a Postmodern World: The Full Conviction of Belief*. Louisville: Westminster John Knox, 1989

Anderson, David. *Multicultural Ministry: Finding your Church's Unique Rhythm*. Grand Rapids: Zondervan, 2004.

Bakke, Ray. *The Urban Christian*. Downers Grove, IL: InterVarsity, 1987.

Balthasar, Hans Urs von. *Prayer*. San Francisco: Ignatius, 1986.

Bass, Dorothy. "Introduction." In *Practicing Theology: Beliefs and Practices in Christian Life*, edited by Dorothy Bass and Miroslav Volf, 1–9. Grand Rapids: Eerdmans, 2002.

Bauman, Zygmunt. *Modernity and the Holocaust*. New York: Ithaca, 1999.

——. *Community: Seeking Safety in an Insecure World*. Malden, MA: Polity, 2001.

——. *Society Under Siege*. Malden, MA: Polity, 2002.

——. *Liquid Love: On the Frailty of Human Bonds*. Malden, MA: Polity, 2003.

Bell, Daniel M. *Liberation Theology after the End of History: The Refusal to Cease Suffering*. New York: Routledge, 2001.

Bibby, Reginald W. *Fragmented Gods: The Poverty and Potential of Religion in Canada*. Toronto: Irwin, 1987.

——. *Mosaic Madness: The Poverty and Potential of Life in Canada*. Toronto: Stoddart, 1990.

Bissoondath, Neil. *Selling Illusions: The Cult of Multiculturalism in Canada*. Toronto: Penguin, 2000.

Boff, Leonardo. *Saint Francis: A Model for Human Liberation*. Translated by John Diercksmeier. New York: Crossroads, 1984.

Borg, Marcus, and N. T. Wright. *The Meaning of Jesus: Two Visions*. San Francisco: HarperSanFrancisco, 1999.

Bosch, David J. *Transforming Mission: Paradigm Shifts in Theology of Missions*. Maryknoll, NY: Orbis, 1991.

Bouma-Prediger, Steven, and Brian J. Walsh. *Beyond Homelessness: Christian Faith in a Culture of Displacement*. Grand Rapids: Eerdmans, 2008.

Bruggemann, Walter. *Interpretation and Obedience: From Faithful Reading to Faithful Living*. Edited by Patrick D. Miller. Minneapolis: Fortress, 1991.

——. *The Prophetic Imagination*. Minneapolis: Fortress, 1978.

Butler Bass, Diana. *Christianity For the Rest of Us How the Neighborhood Church Is Transforming the Faith.* San Francisco: HarperSanFrancisco, 2006.

Catford, Cheryl, editor. *Following Fire: How the Spirit Leads us to Fight Injustice.* Springvale, Victoria: Urban Neighbours of Hope, 2008.

Chittister, Joan. *Wisdom Distilled from the Daily: Living the Rule of St. Benedict Today.* San Francisco: HarperSanFrancisco, 1991.

Chrysostom. "Homily 45." In *St. Chrysostom: Homilies on Acts of the Apostles.* Nicene and Post-Nicene Fathers 1. Edinburgh: T. & T. Clark, 1991.

Chu, Bill. "Abandoned Dinner Led To Understanding." *B. C. Christian News*, September 27, 1996.

Claiborne, Shane. *The Irresistible Revolution: Living as an Ordinary Radical.* Grand Rapids: Zondervan, 2006.

————. "Sharing Economic Resources with Fellow Community Members and the Needy Among Us." In *School(s) for Conversion: 12 Marks of a New Monasticism*, edited by The Rutba House, 26–38. New Monastic Library 1. Eugene, OR: Cascade Books, 2002.

Clapp, Rodney. *Families at the Crossroads: Beyond Traditional and Modern Options.* Downers Grove, IL: InterVarsity, 1999.

Coggins, Jim. "The State of the Canadian Church: A Nation of Believers?" December 6, 2007. Online: http://www.canadianchristianity.com/nationalupdates/071206state .html.

Cox, Harvey. "The Market as God." *The Atlantic Monthly* (March 1999) 18–24.

Crohn, Joel. *Mixed Marriages: How to Create Successful Interracial, Interethnic and Interfaith Relationships.* New York: Fawcett, 1995.

Diehl, William E. *Thank God, It's Monday.* Laity Exchange Books. Minneapolis: Fortress, 1982.

Dorrell, Jimmy. "Pass the Potatoes, Please." In *Hospitality*, edited by Robert B. Kruschwitz, 71–74. Christian Reflection. Waco, TX: The Center for Christian Ethics, Baylor University, 2007.

Dykstra, Craig, and Dorothy Bass. "A Theological Understanding of Christian Practices." In *Practicing Theology: Beliefs and Practices in Christian Life*, 13–32. Edited by Dorothy Bass and Miroslav Volf. Grand Rapids: Eerdmans, 2002.

Elliot, John H. *A Home for the Homeless: A Sociological Exegesis of 1 Peter, Its Situation and Strategy.* 1990. Reprint, Eugene, OR: Wipf & Stock, 2005.

Evdokimov, Paul. *Ages of the Spiritual Life.* Translated by Michel Plekon and Elexis Vinogradov. 1990. Crestwood, NY: St. Valdaimir's Seminary Press.

Galindo, Israel. *Staying Put: A Look at the First Ten Years of Ministry.* Herndon, VA: Alban Institute, 2007.

Greater Vancouver Homelessness Count Bulletin. Online: http://www.gvrd.bc.ca/ homelessness/research.htm.

Grenz, Stanley J. *A Primer on Postmodernism.* Downers Grove, IL: InterVarsity, 1992.

————. *Renewing the Center: Evangelical Theology in a Post-Theological Era.* Grand Rapids: Baker, 2000.

————. *The Social God and the Relational Self: A Trinitarian Theology of the Imago Dei.* Louisville: Westminster John Knox, 2004.

Grenz, Stanley J., and Roger Olson. *Twentieth-Century Theology: God and the World in a Transitional Age.* Downers Grove, IL: InterVarsity, 1992.

Guder, Daryl. *The Continuing Conversion of the Church*. Grand Rapids: Eerdmans, 2000.

Gutierrez, Gustavo. *A Theology of Liberation*. Maryknoll, NY: Orbis, 1973.

———. *We Drink From our Own Wells: The Spiritual Journey of a People*. Maryknoll, NY: Orbis, 1984.

Hauerwas, Stanley. *The Peaceable Kingdom: A Primer in Christian Ethics*. Notre Dame: University of Notre Dame Press, 1983.

Hays, Richard B. *The Moral Vision of the New Testament: Community, Cross, New Creation*. San Francisco: HarperSanFrancisco, 1996.

Inge, John. *A Christian Theology of Place*. London: Ashgate, 2003.

Janzen, David. "Intentional Formation in the Way of Christ and the Rule of the Community Along the lines of the Old Novitiate." In *School(s) for Conversion: 12 Marks of a New Monasticism*, edited by Rutba House. New Monastic Library 1. Eugene, OR: Cascade Books, 2002.

Jenkins, Philip. *The Next Christendom: The Coming of Global Christianity*. New York: Oxford University Press, 2002.

Jersak, Brad. "Interview with Dave Diewert." *Clarion: Journal of Spirituality and Justice*. June 9, 2006. Online: http://clarionjournal.typepad.com/clarion_journal_of_spirit/2006/06/safe_injection_.html.

Jones, L. Gregory. "A Thirst for God or Consumer Spirituality: Cultivating Disciplined Practices of Being Engaged by God." *Modern Theology* 13 (2000) 3–28.

Justin, the Martyr. "The First Apology of Justin the Martyr." In *Early Christian Fathers*, edited by Cyril C. Richardson. San Francisco: Ignatius, 2002.

Kauffman, Ivan. "Humble Submission to Christ's Body, The Church." In *School(s) for Conversion: 12 Marks of a New Monasticism*, edited by Rutba House, 68–79. New Monastic Library 1. Eugene, OR: Cascade Books, 2002.

Kenneson, Phillip D. *Life on the Vine: Cultivating the Fruit of the Spirit in Christian Community*. Downers Grove, IL: InterVarsity, 1999.

Kunstler, James Howard. *Geography of Nowhere: The Rise and Decline of America's Man-Made Landscape*. New York: Simon & Schuster, 1994.

LeClerq, Jean. *Monks and Love in Twelfth Century France: Psycho-historical Essays*. Oxford: Clarendon, 1979.

Leech, Kenneth. *Soul Friend: An Invitation to Spiritual Direction*. New York: Harper Collins, 1992.

Lovelace, Richard. *Dynamics of Spiritual Life: An Evangelical Theology of Renewal*. Downers Grove, IL: InterVarsity, 1979.

MacIntyre, Alasdair. *After Virtue: A Study in Moral Theory*. 2nd ed. Notre Dame: University of Notre Dame Press. 1984.

McGavran, Donald A. *Understanding Church Growth*. 3rd ed. Grand Rapids: Eerdmans, 1990.

McLellan, Janet, and Richard H. Anthony. "Multiculturalism in Crisis: A Postmodern Perspective in Canada." *Ethnic and Racial Studies* 17 (1990) 662–83.

Merton, Thomas. *New Seeds of Contemplation*. New York: Doubleday, 1969.

Middleton, Richard, and Brian Walsh. *Truth is Stranger than it Used to Be: Biblical Truth in a Postmodern Age*. Downers Grove: InterVarsity,1984.

Milne, Bruce. *Dynamic Diversity: Bridging Class, Age, Race and Gender in the Church*. Nottingham, UK: InterVarsity, 2006.

Moltmann, Jürgen. *The Coming of God: Christian Eschatology*. Translated by Margaret Kohl. Minneapolis: Fortress, 1996.

Newbigin, Lesslie. *Foolishness to the Greeks: The Gospel and Western Culture.* Grand Rapids: Eerdmans, 1986.

———. *The Gospel in a Pluralist Society.* Grand Rapids: Eerdmans, 1989.

Newman, Elizabeth. *Untamed Hospitality: Welcoming God and Other Strangers.* Grand Rapids: Brazos, 2007.

Norris, Kathleen. *The Cloister Walk.* New York: Riverhead, 1996.

Pascal, Blaise. *Pensees.* Translated by A. J. Krailsheimer. New York: Penguin. 1996.

Palmer, Parker J. *Let your Life Speak: Listening for the Voice of Vocation.* San Francisco: Jossey-Bass, 2000.

Payne, Leanne. *The Healing Presence.* Wheaton, IL: Crossway, 1989.

Pearce, Paul. "Characteristics of Emerging Healthy Multicultural Churches." DMin thesis, McMaster Divinity College, 2000.

Pennington, Basil. *A School of Love: The Cistercian Way to Holiness.* Harrisburg, PA: Morehouse, 2001.

Perkins, John. *With Justice For All.* Ventura, CA: Regal, 1982.

Perkins, Spencer, and Chris Rice. *More Than Equals: Racial Healing for the Sake of the Gospel.* Downers Grove: InterVarsity, 1993.

Peterson, Eugene. *The Contemplative Pastor.* Grand Rapids: Eerdmans, 1993.

Plantinga, Alvin. *Warranted Christian Belief.* New York: Oxford University Press, 2000.

Plantinga Pauw, Amy. "Attending to the Gap between Beliefs and Practices." In *Practicing Theology: Beliefs and Practices in Christian Life,* edited by Dorothy Bass and Miroslav Volf, 33–49. Grand Rapids: Eerdmans, 2002.

Plantinga, Cornelius. *Not the Way It's Supposed to Be: A Breviary of Sin.* Grand Rapids: Eerdmans, 1995.

Pohl, Christine. *Making Room: Recovering Hospitality as a Christian Tradition.* Grand Rapids: Eerdmans, 1999.

Putnam, Robert. "Bowling Alone: America's Declining Social Capital." *Journal of American Democracy* 6 (1995) 65–78.

Randall, Debora. *Research on Economic Needs and Development Opportunities.* Vancouver: Salsbury Community Society, 2003.

Rice, Chris. "Lamenting Racial Divisions." In *School(s) for Conversion: 12 Marks of a New Monasticism,* edited by Rutba House, 55–67. New Monastic Library 1. Eugene, OR: Cascade Books, 2002.

Ricouer, Paul. *The Conflict of Interpretations: Essays in Hermeneutics.* Translated by Willis Domingo. Edited by Don Ihde. Evanston, IL: Northwestern University Press, 1969.

Ringma, Charles. "Liberation Theologians Speak to Evangelicals: A Theology and Praxis of Serving the Poor." Draft of a paper presented to the Asian Theological Society, 2008.

———. *Seek the Silences with Thomas Merton: Reflections on Identity, Community and Transformative Action.* Vancouver: Regent College Publishing, 2003.

Rolheiser, Ronald. *The Holy Longing: A Search for a Christian Spirituality.* New York: Doubleday, 1999.

———. *The Shattered Lantern.* New York: Crossroads, 2003.

Romero, Oscar. *The Violence of Love.* 2nd ed. Farmington, PA: Plough, 1998.

The Rutba House, editor. *School(s) for Conversion: 12 Marks of a New Monasticism.* Eugene, OR: Cascade, 2002.

Schultze, Quentin. *Habits of the High Tech Heart: Living Virtuously in an Age of Technology.* Grand Rapids: Baker, 2002.

Sobrino, Jon. *Witnesses to the Kingdom: The Martyrs of El Salvador and the Crucified Peoples*. Maryknoll, NY: Orbis, 2003.

Sofield, Loughlan, Rosine Hammett, and Carroll Juliano. *Building Community: Christian, Caring, Vital*. Notre Dame, IN: Ave Maria, 1998.

St. John of the Cross. *The Complete Works of St. John of the Cross*. Translated and edited by E. Allison Peers. 3rd ed. Westminster, MD: Newman, 1953.

Taylor, Charles. *Sources of the Self: The Making of the Modern Identity*. Cambridge: Harvard University Press, 1989.

———. *A Secular Age*. Cambridge: Belnap, 2007.

Vanier, Jean. *Becoming Human*. New York: Paulist, 1999.

———. *Community and Growth*. New York: Paulist, 1979.

Volf, Miroslav. *The End of Memory: Remembering Rightly in a Violent World*. Grand Rapids: Eerdmans, 2006.

———. *Exclusion and Embrace: A Theological Exploration into Identity and Otherness*. Nashville: Abingdon, 1996.

———. "Theology as a Way of Life." In *Practicing Theology: Beliefs and Practices in Christian Life*, edited by Miroslav Volf and Dorothy C. Bass, 245–63. Grand Rapids: Eerdmans, 2002.

Volf, Miroslav, and Dorothy Bass, editors. *Practicing Theology: Beliefs and Practices in Christian Life*. Grand Rapids: Eerdmans, 2002.

Weil, Simone. *The Need for Roots: Prelude to a Declaration of Duties towards Mankind*. Translated by A. F. Wills. London: Routledge & Kegan Paul, 1987.

———. *Waiting for God*. New York: Putnam, 1951.

Wilson, Jonathan R. *Living Faithfully in a Fragmented World: Lessons for the Church from MacIntyre's After Virtue*. Hartsburg, PA: Trinity, 1997.

———. *Why Church Matters: Worship, Ministry and Mission in Practice*. Grand Rapids: Brazos, 2006.

Wilson-Hartgrove, Jonathan. "The Beatitudes in the Desert." In *Sermon on the Mount*, edited by Robert Kruschwitz, 60–67. Christian Reflections. Waco, TX: The Center for Christian Ethics, Balyor University, 2008.

Wolter, Maurus. *Principles of Monasticism*. Translated by Bernard A. Sause. St. Louis: Herder, 1962.

Wolterstorff, Nicholas. "The Grace That Shaped My Life." In *Philosophers Who Believe: The Spiritual Journeys of 11 Leading Thinkers*, edited by Kelly James Clark, 259–76. Downers Grove, IL: InterVarsity, 1999.

———. *Justice: Rights and Wrongs*. Princeton: Princeton University Press, 2008.

———. *Until Justice and Peace Embrace*. Grand Rapids: Eerdmans, 1986.

Wright, N. T. *Evil and the Justice of God*. Downers Grove, IL: InterVarsity, 2006.

———. *Jesus and the Victory of God*. Christian Origins and the Question of God 2. Minneapolis: Fortress, 1996.

———. *The New Testament and the People of God*. Christian Origins and the Question of God 1. Minneapolis: Fortress, 1992.

———. *Paul*. Minneapolis: Fortress, 2005.

———. *The Resurrection of the Son of God*. Christian Origins and the Question of God 3. Minneapolis: Fortress, 2003.

———. *Simply Christian: Why Christianity Makes Sense*. New York: HarperCollins, 2006.

———. *Surprised by Hope: Rethinking Heaven, the Resurrection, and the Mission of the Church*. New York: HarperCollins., 2008.

Yancey, George. *One Body, One Spirit: Principles of Successful Multiracial Churches.* Downers Grove, IL: InterVarsity, 2003.

Zizioulous, John. *Being in Communion.* Crestwood, NY: St. Vladamir's Seminary Press, 1985.